# Expect Great Things

Also by Richard W. O'Ffill

*Transforming Prayer*

To order, call 1-800-765-6955.
Visit our Web site at *www.reviewandherald.com* for information on other Review and Herald products.

RICHARD W. O'FFILL

# Expect Great Things

## HOW TO BE A HAPPY, GROWING CHRISTIAN

**ІІ**

REVIEW AND HERALD® PUBLISHING ASSOCIATION
HAGERSTOWN, MD 21740

The author assumes full responsibility for the accuracy of all facts
and quotations as cited in this book.


This book was
Edited by Gerald Wheeler
Copyedited by Jocelyn Fay and James Cavil
Designed by Kimberly Haupt
Electronic makeup by Shirley M. Bolivar
Cover art by Tony Stone Images and Kimberly Haupt
Typeset: 12/15 Bembo


PRINTED IN U.S.A.

05  04  03  02  01          5  4  3  2  1


**R&H Cataloging Service**
O'Ffill, Richard Wesley, 1940–
        Expect great things.

        1. Christian life. I. Title.

            248.386732




ISBN-0-8280-1512-0

# *Dedication*

This book is dedicated to the loving memory of my mother. She was the one who brought me to Jesus. My mother taught me to pray, and for that I will forever be thankful.

# Contents

# *What to Expect From This Book*

There is no such thing as the Christian life made easy. Accessible, doable, and successful yes—but easy? I don't think so. Although Scripture teaches that the way of the transgressor is hard (Prov. 13:15), in other places it compares the Christian life to a race (Heb. 12:1), a fight (1 Tim. 6:12), and a wrestling match (Eph. 6:12). It tells stories of the faithful who endured persecution and gave their lives along the way. In Scripture we read of winners and of losers. Our Saviour even warned us that inasmuch as He had suffered while He was here we could expect the same (John 15:20). We need to understand this, because so much of how we relate to something depends on our expectations beforehand. If our assumptions as to how something is supposed to be do not reflect reality, we can easily become discouraged and may even be tempted to give up.

In addition, that reality must be founded on God's design. We must resist the temptation to create expectations that we invent for ourselves.

Real-life experience constantly reminds us that though the gospel may be simple, it is not easy to implement. Also I have concluded that although the gospel is easy, error is definitely difficult and confusing. The problems that many seem to struggle with as they implement the gospel in their lives correspond to their unreal expectations and/or misinformation. Once we strip error away and see things the way they were meant to be, we will then be more effective in our spiritual race.

If the Christian life is to be successful in the sense that it represents God's will, it must not be something we do piecemeal. Although the Christian life has many components, it really forms only one whole. An attempt to implement one part and knowingly omit another will ultimately lead to frustration and uneven spiritual growth.

When my son and his wife moved they decided they needed more furniture. I don't recall exactly what they bought, but I do remember that he asked me if furniture had always come disassembled the way so much of it does now. I told him I didn't think so but that if he would follow the directions he would have no trouble putting the pieces together. The box usually has a picture of what the object will finally look like along with step-by-step assembly instructions inside. Without the picture and the instructions a person might eventually figure it all out, but I would be interested to see the creative variations that might occur.

In order to know where all the pieces fit in the Christian life a person needs to have the big picture of what it is supposed to look like as they go along. This book is about what to expect in your Christian life. When we each have our own individual idea of the Christian life, two things can happen. One is that our concept could become a self-fulfilling prophecy, and the other is that it may not seem to work the way we thought it would.

We don't need to worry, however. It is not necessary or advisable to play the Christian life by ear and see what just happens, nor do we have to go through life convinced we are a factory reject. There is hope, but we do have to follow some definite assembly instructions.

If you are a carpenter, or at least have had a measuring tape and saw in your hands, you have no doubt had the experience I am about to describe. Let's suppose that for some reason a task in the workshop requires eight pieces of wood, all of the same length. They must each be 11 and three-quarters inches in length. So you take the tape and measure 11 and three-quarters inches on the board. You find a straight edge and cut the first piece. It suddenly occurs to you that you don't have to measure the other seven pieces—you will use the one you cut as a template. So you cut the second piece. Then you reach for the third board and are about to use the second piece as a template for the third. Wait! Stop! Don't do it. You know what will happen, don't you? If you use the last-cut piece to cut the next, by the time you have your eight pieces they will definitely not all measure 11 and three-quarters inches. Each one will have shrunk by at least the width of the saw blade.

It works the same way in the Christian life. When everyone uses their own measuring tape, pretty soon they begin to get all kinds of results. That is why to avoid being frustrated in the Christian life we must start by using an objective measure, and you may already have guessed what that is. The Bible is the measuring tape of the Christian life. Scripture pictures for us how things are supposed to be. When a person gets the big picture, the pieces that make up the everyday things of life will have a place to fit in.

Have you ever taken something apart only to discover when you got it back together that you had parts left over? On one occasion I changed the fluid in my car's transmission, and when I finished I had a little ball bearing with no home. *Oh, well,* I thought, *everything else fits just fine and the ball bearing is just a little one.* But when I started up the car for a test drive, you can guess what happened.

If the Christian life is going to work as it is supposed to, we need to have all the pieces in the right places. I would not say that people who are putting together their lives in Christ must wait until they have all the pieces assembled at one time, but it is definitely necessary that the pieces that are in place are in the right spot, and it is not advisable purposely to leave some parts out.

In this book we are not going see how little we can make the pieces. After all is said and done, it is the big picture that we are after, not the parts (though we must not forget that they do comprise the picture). We are going to come at it from what I will call a modular approach. Though each module itself consists of many pieces, we won't try to make it difficult by taking the module apart, but will try simply to show where each module fits in and how each one relates to the rest. Later if you want to take each module apart, feel free to do so. But I suspect we have been into that too much already. This is probably why many people don't ever seem to get it all together and end up either settling for something less than the best or become frustrated and conclude that in the here and now you just can't get there from here.

If our expectations are going to be correct, we must begin with the big picture of what the Christian life involves. All the pieces must belong to this picture. One biblical passage sets the parameters and gives an overview of the Christian life. While I recognize that some people are not comfortable with establishing a doctrine with one Bible text (and neither am I), I don't think you will argue with this particular one. We can say it a thousand ways with a thousand texts, but I don't believe it could be said better or clearer.

Romans 8:29 declares: "For whom he did foreknow, he also did predestinate to be conformed to the image of his Son, that he might be firstborn among many brethren." In plain language it is saying that the purpose of the Christian life is that we will be like Jesus.

To be successful as a Christian we must understand that if we head in one direction when God wants us to go another, we will only have problems. Knowing what God's plan is for our life will also cut out a lot of extraneous concerns we might otherwise have. As long as we can see the picture on the box (as when we buy a piece of unassembled furniture) we can know even when we start how it is supposed to turn out in the end. Then as we follow the assembly directions we can continually refer to the picture to confirm that we are indeed on the right track. That is why we must keep before us the picture of Jesus as we pursue the Christian life.

So that we will all be literally reading from the same page, it is important to understand that I begin with the premise that God has provided a perfect plan of salvation. Therefore, I will focus on how we should relate to that salvation.

An American evangelist in Ethiopia scheduled a series of meetings to last several weeks. He had the titles of each lecture all made up. Apparently they were the ones he used when he conducted meetings in the Western world. One of the sermon titles was: "Is There a God?" A local minister glanced at the title and said, "You might as well leave that sermon out. Whether or not there is a God is no issue in this country."

This book assumes that those who read it want the salvation God offers, but at times they appreciate encouragement as to how each piece of the puzzle relates to the others and how they all fit together.

The chapters of this book touch on real life. As a minister I am sensitive to the fact that when we talk about the spiritual life we often speak another language—or at least a vocabulary and frame of reference generally not understood by the person in the street or even, for that matter, in the pew.

A little boy sat listening to a famous preacher. The child had looked forward to hearing the person and knew that what he was hearing must be a wonderful sermon. The trouble was that it was over his head. As he wiggled there frustrated, he mumbled to himself, "Put the cookies on the lower shelf, Pastor; put the cookies on the lower shelf!"

It is my prayer that this book will put the cookies on the lower shelf without cheapening them or breaking them. If you have wanted your life in Christ to be more meaningful, or if there have been some pieces of the gospel that haven't always seemed to fit together, I hope you will be inspired and encouraged. And when you have finished may God have revitalized you in a special way as you continue to grow in grace and in the knowledge of our Lord and Saviour Jesus Christ.

## What Is Important to Know

1. There is no such thing as an easy Christian life.

2. Misplaced expectations about the Christian life can lead to frustration and discouragement.

3. A successful Christian life comes when we can see the big picture—being like Jesus. Once we have this overview we can learn where each of the pieces of the puzzle fits and how they relate to each other.

## Personal Application

1. What do you think it means to live the Christian life piecemeal? What will be the result?

2. Do you think it is necessary to have all the pieces of the Christian life in hand before you can begin to put the picture together? Explain your answer.

## Prayer

Heavenly Father, we thank You that in Jesus Christ we can have full salvation. Lord, we are thankful for Your Word, which is like having a flashlight when we are in the dark. We knew error before we knew the truth. As we begin this reading, we ask that the Holy Spirit make His light shine brightly in our hearts and minds. Just as light imprints a picture on a piece of film, may Jesus' life be printed on the film of our hearts that we might indeed be conformed to His image. Amen.

# Expect to Put the Past Behind You

Someone has said that if you want to stop your enemies from getting their ideas across simply take over their language. You make their words now have new meanings—yours. The devil has always employed this strategy with great success.

A catchall word that many use these days to describe the Christian life is relationship. Society urges everyone to have a relationship with Jesus. Needless to say, responding to an invitation to have a relationship with Jesus at first glance seems easy, because the word "relationship" is generic. It would not be stretching the truth to say that everyone already has a relationship with Jesus, including the devil (he hates Him).

Once I talked with a young man who was living with his girlfriend. Trying to justify the arrangement, he explained that they were best friends, loved each other, shared expenses, and found intimacy with each other.

"Hey," I responded, "that sounds like my wife and me. Why don't you go ahead and get married?"

He shook his head. "No," he replied, "we don't want to make a commitment."

The young person was willing to have a relationship, but making a commitment was out of the question.

Because things are often not what they appear to be, it has trivialized the language. As a result it has made it increasingly difficult to communicate to people what it means to be a Christian and what we can expect the Christian life to be like. Since modern society has emptied "relationship" of much of its meaning, we should not consider it the ultimate word in describing why we come to Christ or how we live a life in which we become more and more like Him. Scripture does not attempt to portray how the Christian life begins and how it proceeds using just one word. For us to do so does not give the big picture and can even lead to misplaced expectations.

The Bible uses two concepts to explain how the new life in Christ begins. The same concepts also apply to the ongoing process. One is that we must be crucified with Christ (Gal. 2:19, 20). The other is that we must be born again (John 3:3; 1 Peter 1:23). Both concepts are foundational to the Christian life. If we leave them out or somehow figure they are automatic and we don't have to think about them, either we will end up with a lot of pieces left over, or we will run out of pieces before we finish the picture.

People today do not really understand the concept of crucifixion. Most people think of the cross as little more than an ornament or even a decoration. But the Roman Empire used crucifixion as the death penalty for what it considered the worst possible crimes, and as a terrorist weapon to destroy all resistance to its power. The Roman authorities deliberately made crucifixion as horrible and disgusting as possible, filling it with public disgrace. It is impossible to describe a typical crucifixion because of the many variations. The Roman writer Seneca said that he had seen not just one kind of cross but many. Executioners crucified some victims upside down, impaled some through their private parts, and crucified still others with their arms stretched out on the crossbeams. The victim's family and friends could not even show grief over the person's fate. If they did, the soldiers would immediately execute them, too. As a final insult, the bodies were not allowed burial. They either had to rot on the cross as a public warning or be tossed into a river. Whoever asked for the body of a crucified person risked his or her own death.

When Jesus tells us to take up our cross and follow Him (Matt. 16:24), or when the apostle Paul declared that we are crucified with Christ (Gal. 2:19), the people in those days understood what it meant. The cross was a symbol of death. For centuries Christians rarely even depicted it. It represented an abrupt, violent, and shameful end of life. A person in ancient Roman times who had a cross loaded on his shoulders and started down the road to the place of crucifixion had already said goodbye to his friends. He would not be coming back. When the cross had finished its work its victim was dead. A person didn't do time on the cross.

Unfortunately we hear little preaching of the cross today. And when we do, it is often not the old cross that Jesus spoke of and that Paul and his contemporaries understood, one that brought death to the victim. It is now common to hear about a new cross. Instead of killing a person, the new cross redirects them. While the cross of ancient Roman times stripped its victims and exposed them to public humiliation, the cross of modern times endeavors to maintain self-respect.

If we are to understand what it means to become a follower of Christ, we must grasp the significance of crucifixion. It means that one kind of life has to end if we are going to begin another. To use computer terminology, the Christian life is not simply installing another program along with all the others that may exist on life's hard drive. It means a complete reformatting of the disk itself. The cross makes clear the meaning of the words: "Old things are passed away; behold, all things are become new" (2 Cor. 5:17). Though it is possible to gradually adopt some new lifestyle, we cannot ease into a new life in Christ. It requires a radical end of an old way of life. When we understand the meaning of crucifixion, we know that the Christian life cannot be an add-on. It must be a new beginning. The new life in Christ is not an enhancement of the old (Rom. 6:4-6). For this reason we should not try to see how much the new life is similar to the old, but rather examine the ways in which it is different.

Christ's concept of being born again reinforces the idea of the Christian life as a new beginning. Just as they do not often emphasize being crucified with Christ, so many churches tend to ignore being born again, though we do hear a lot about "getting saved." A man once mentioned to me that he had been saved 23 times. When Jesus talked that night with Nicodemus, He told him that to get saved we have to be born again. Nicodemus thought that Jesus was referring to biology instead of theology, so he immediately corrected the Lord by declaring that would not be possible (John 3:4).

It was then that Jesus let him know they were not in Biology 101 but in Theology 101. The point Jesus made and what Paul meant when he referred to crucifixion is that the Christian life is not a continuation of the old life. When we commit our lives to Jesus, we don't take up where we left off.

Of course, when we come to Jesus we bring all the baggage we have collected throughout our lives. Such baggage has grown unbearable. We would not have any reason to accept Jesus unless we are fed up with the status quo. Until a person finally realizes that pride, selfishness, bitterness and resentment, lust, and lack of self-control are no longer acceptable, they will have little motivation to change.

As we think of all of life's accumulated baggage, suddenly what Jesus said about the gate being narrow and the road being narrow begins to get pretty exciting (Matt. 7:14). Have you ever come to a turnstile while carrying suitcases in both hands? Although you may not need your hands to get through a turnstile, you definitely can't get through holding on to luggage. You have to let go.

This is wonderful news. The concepts of being crucified and born again are truly liberating, because they signify a new start. It means that though the past may have been unbearable, it is behind us now. The Christian life is not about living in the past. The crucifixion takes care of that. When Jesus told Nicodemus that the gospel consists of being born again, that means we don't have to be trapped in what happened in the past.

But here is where some Christians get stuck. Many beliefs in the world tell us that in order to go forward we must journey backward. But that is not what the New Testament model of the life in Christ teaches. When my oldest daughter was in the academy she took driver's education. One day she came home from class and told me something I have never forgotten. "Daddy," she said to me, "today our driver's education teacher told us that what we see is what we hit."

The magazine of the American Automobile Association once featured an article entitled "The Moth Effect." It explained why thousands of accidents each year involve a moving car crashing into a vehicle parked along the side of the road. The author pointed out that as light attracts a moth, so a person tends to travel in the direction in which they are looking. The implications for the Christian life are obvious. What we see is what we hit. We move in the direction in which we are looking. If in our lives we are looking backward, we will sooner or later begin to go in that direction (Luke 9:62).

Raised in a minister's home, I am thankful that we children were able to attend church schools and a Christian college. Not everyone has those same opportunities. Many have grown up in a non-Christian environment. If you happen to be one of those whose past is sad and even painful, I would like to encourage you—and even, if you don't mind, tease you. What difference does it really make whether your dad was a minister or someone who wasn't interested in religion? Jesus said we must all be born again anyway.

First John 3:2 reminds us that having been crucified with Christ and born again by His Spirit, we now know that we are God's sons and daughters. Although we don't yet know everything that God has planned for us, when He returns to earth, no matter the past, we will be like Him, for we will see Him as He is.

### What Is Important to Know

1. The Christian life is not a continuation of the past. Being crucified with Christ and being born again changes us.

2. The Christian life crashes like an overloaded computer when we regard Jesus as an add-on. Spiritually speaking, what we see is what we hit. If we spend time looking back at the wrongs we have committed and that have been done against us, we will find it difficult to grow spiritually.

### Personal Application

1. Being crucified and born again does not make such things as a divorce go away. How does a person who has a new life in Christ relate to his or her past?

2. Get a pen and paper or go to the computer and write in your own words what it will look like in your life to be crucified with Christ.

### Prayer

Dear God, we have a lot in our past that is pretty bad. It has made us angry, and it is easy to be bitter and resentful against those who have wronged us. We even get discouraged with our own past mistakes and sometimes feel hopeless. Now we can see that in the death, burial, and resurrection of Jesus we can get a new start. But the truth is, Lord, we sometimes prefer things as they are rather than the possibility that You have given us to forgive, be forgiven, and forget.

As we remember Jesus' crucifixion and resurrection, may the Holy Spirit take us in faith to be there with Him in His crucifixion so that we can forget the past and begin a new life. Thank You that Jesus is not only our hope, but through the Holy Spirit He is our help. Amen.

# *Expect to Be Held Accountable*

In the last chapter we pointed out that the devil continually redefines the words we use to convey spiritual truth.

Because of this, we must be careful to do two things. First, we must continually remind ourselves of the biblical meaning of words. This is necessary, because if we apply new definitions to the words in Scripture, we will find that we have changed the meaning of the message.

Second, we must not attempt to reduce the truth to sound bites. In other words, we should not try to see how briefly we can explain salvation. Salvation is not buzzwords. For example, we could say that in order to drive a car all a person has to do is get in and turn the key. Although that would be true, it would not present all that driving involves, and I don't need to tell you what could happen if you got into a car knowing nothing more than that.

God inspired the writing of the Bible so that when we get the big picture, we get the right picture. We must remind ourselves that while we may throw away the box and packing material that a new piece of unassembled furniture comes in, we should never discard anything from the Word of God.

If we were starting from scratch, it would not be so difficult for us to understand what the gospel is and how it works. But because erroneous concepts and misunderstandings so permeate our minds, God has graciously brought us His Word from a number of different perspectives. Although they approach the topic from different angles, they never contradict one another. They are all pieces of the puzzle, and as we get them together and in the right place we will find that many of our frustrations in Christian living disappear. Doors that before seemed nailed shut will now swing open.

Some express concern that we have been too negative in our concepts of the Christian life. Whether something is negative or positive should not worry us, but rather whether it is true or false. When the serpent told Eve that if she ate of the tree of knowledge of good and evil she would not die (Gen. 3:4), the statement was positive, but it was also a lie. On the other hand, when God said that if they ate of the tree they would die (Gen. 2:17), what He told Adam and Eve was negative yet completely true.

A vital biblical word seems to have vanished in recent years—repentance. Repentance speaks of something fundamental to a growing and dynamic Christian life, yet some react uncomfortably to it, because of the spin that others have put on it. They regard the word "repentance" as too negative. Yet repentance is indispensable to commencing the Christian walk, and then it enables a person to grow in grace and spiritual knowledge.

In my early days I used to be a plasterer. In the plastering process we first apply a base coat of plaster to the wall. When that is dry, we mix finely crushed lime into a paste. The lime will become an ingredient in the finish coat. Normally a pure lime mix on the wall will dry out but will not set up and form a hard surface. To make that possible we add a small can of plaster of Paris to five gallons of the lime mix. When we spread and smooth the mixture it gives the wall the firm surface we need.

Like plaster of Paris, repentance is the component that we must continually add to the Christian life if we are to acquire the finish God desires of us. Remember, the purpose of the gospel is to make us like Jesus. While many today consider repentance a put-down, it is interesting to note that during the revivals of the eighteenth and nineteenth centuries preachers based their call for people to come to Jesus on a summons to repent. During the past 100 years or so, instead of urging people to repent, the approach has been to invite them to come to Jesus to improve their lifestyle.

This emphasis is a relatively new phenomenon. In the Old Testament the message of the prophets was to repent. When Jesus began His ministry His theme was "Repent: for the kingdom of heaven is at hand" (Matt. 4:17). John the Baptist pleaded for his hearers to repent (Matt. 3:2). Peter on the day of Pentecost preached, "Repent ye therefore, and be converted, that your sins may be blotted out" (Acts 3:19). The great revivals in Europe and America were all based on a call to repentance. When rightly understood, repentance is not a put-down word but a summons to change. It means that we don't need to let the past continue to drag us down. If we will only experience repentance, we can get a new start.

Today a call to acceptance has largely replaced the command for repentance. It may seem to some that it is merely another way of saying the same thing, but acceptance tends to infer status quo while repentance demands change. While acceptance is a good word, it can acquire a connotation that may actually block what the Holy Spirit is trying to do in our lives. If you want someone to work for you, how would you feel if they said, "If you decide to hire me, I need to tell you now that you are going to have to accept me just the way I am." It could sound as though they are not willing to improve their professional skills.

Inasmuch as the Christian life begins with the death of the old life and then goes on to a new birth, change is very much what the gospel is all about. When rightly understood, the Christian life is hardly what a person would call being stuck in a rut.

The story of the prodigal son makes it clear (Luke 15:22). The young man came home to his father just as he was. His father received him just as he was. But he didn't accept him just as he was, because he smelled like a pig. It wasn't long before the young man had a bath and clean clothes. Each of us must come to Jesus just as we are for the simple reason that we can't do it any other way. We don't take a shower before we get into the shower, but step into it in the condition we happen to be in. But when we get out of the shower we are not the same way we were before. So God receives us just as we are, but when we come to Him wonderful changes begin to take place.

Given the current social climate and the spin-doctoring that the devil is doing to the gospel vocabulary, I have concluded that it would leave no room for confusion if, instead of saying that God accepts us and we ought to accept each other, we used the term *receive*. God receives us as we are, and so too we should receive each other.

Another word has recently entered the mix: "dysfunction." This word can make repentance seem to be unnecessary. I do not deny the existence of what we refer to as dysfunction or the impact it has in our lives. Dysfunction is real. Unless we deal with dysfunction it will continue to warp and twist future generations.

The problem with some of the current emphasis on dysfunction, with all its hows and whys, is that some use it to place responsibility for what they are on someone else. Typically the mind-set blames all our problems on our parents. All of us are in some way dysfunctional. And we cannot deny that the way we were raised did contribute to what we became. The question we must ask ourselves now, however, is Why are we the way we are at this moment? Wouldn't it be fair to say that what I am today I decided to be?

Here is where the gospel and what it teaches about our past suddenly becomes extremely relevant to our present life. As we have learned, the gospel is not about the past but rather about the present and the future. Being crucified with Christ, born again, and now having a spirit of repentance, we are able to make a break with the past and at last find ourselves set free to begin again. The gospel doesn't deny the past—it simply refuses to let it get us down.

The gospel also does the greatest favor that one could possibly do a human being—it makes us accountable for what we do. We don't hold a poisonous snake accountable for biting someone or a lion for eating cattle. That is the way those animals are. They cannot act any other way. But thank God, He doesn't treat us like animals—He holds us accountable, because we can make moral choices. The word that demonstrates this is repentance, and it makes sense that God would not call anyone to repent who was incapable of being responsible for what he or she did in the past.

He does not ask animals to repent, but He definitely summons the human race to repent. Inasmuch as He created us in His image in the first place, repentance gets us back on track. As long as we allow ourselves to be prisoners of dysfunction and hold everyone but ourselves accountable for what we are, we will have no reason to repent.

Repentance fits perfectly with being crucified with Christ and being born again. It is the handle by which the grace of God reaches down and lifts us out of our dysfunction and gives us a new start. But when we don't respond with a spirit of repentance, God's forgiveness has no place to go, no way of helping us.

In addition, repentance is not just where we begin, but an ongoing characteristic of the Christian walk. A spirit of repentance is our admission before God of our continual dependence on Him. Of course, it does not originate within ourselves, but is a gift from God (2 Tim. 2:25). He is the source of every good gift and impulse (James 1:17). Thank God for this most wonderful gift of repentance!

In the next two chapters we will learn about two things that short-circuit repentance and make it impossible for it to function.

## What Is Important to Know

1. Repentance transfers us from one way of life to another.

2. Repentance is one thing and acceptance another. They do not mean the same, and we should not use them interchangeably or in place of each other.

3. A continual spirit of repentance is necessary if the Christian is to continue to grow in grace, because it sets him or her free from the past as well as from the status quo.

4. Dysfunction is ultimately what sin is all about. We must not use the concept as a means to avoid personal responsibility.

## Personal Application

1. How can we ensure that we do not perpetuate our past dysfunction into the present?

2. Compare and contrast the concepts expressed by "receiving sinners" and "accepting sinners." How can we be accepting of sinners without being accepting of sin?

## Prayer

Holy Father, thank You that we cannot be in a condition so bad that we can't follow the example of the prodigal son by getting up out of the pigpens of our life and returning home. You have promised that whoever comes to You, You will never cast out. So we come to You as we are, because we cannot do anything else. You are the only one who can clean us from the inside out and restore us to the way You meant for us to be in the beginning.

It is against our nature to admit it when we are wrong, and even when we do, we prefer to blame it on someone else. Please give us the gift of repentance. Help us to see that unless we admit we have been wrong, we will not let You accomplish in our lives what You need to do. Thank You for not being like us. We want to be like You! Amen.

# *Expect to Face Reality*

We live in a culture that wars with what the Holy Spirit seeks to accomplish in our lives. Yet we often expect that truth will be easy to discover and error will be obvious. More likely than not, though, error comes wrapped in a skin of truth that makes it difficult to recognize. But then we should expect this to be the case and should always remain alert. As God's people we need to pray and study that we might have the gift of discernment. Jesus cautioned that the last days would involve deception (Mark 13:5). The apostle Paul even points out that lying would characterize people living in the last days (2 Tim. 3:3).

Lying could well be the worst of all the sins we commit. Without a doubt pride and selfishness are the mother of all sins. But it is the sin of lying that makes all the others possible.

A lie enabled—or we could say facilitated—the very first sin Adam and Eve committed (Gen. 3:4). Thus a lie, in effect, becomes the umbrella under which all the other sins shelter.

The Lord has made it possible for us to break away from and be forgiven of every sin. He says that if we confess our sins He will forgive us and cleanse us from all unrighteousness (1 John 1:9).

The first step toward forgiveness is repentance. As we learned in chapter 2, repentance is to recognize when we have been living contrary to God's will. But unless we are truthful with ourselves, we will never repent. Those who knowingly deny that what they are doing or about to do is against God's will, will continue to disobey.

Overall, honesty is in decline. When I was a little boy my mother used to say, "Dickie, better to die than to tell a lie." Few people would take such an approach today. Many people who should know better have allowed themselves to get into the habit of lying. For many lying has even become a way of life. We may not like to admit it, but if we are in the habit of not always telling the truth we are, in fact, liars. People who tell lies regularly do not see themselves as liars but like to say they are only being politically correct or are putting a different spin on something. When confronted with facts, they might even say they were only kidding or really didn't mean it.

Still others have formed the habit of telling what they consider to be little white lies. They regard such lies as harmless, or if not harmless, at least a better alternative at the time than telling the truth. However, the Bible does not classify lies, so there is really no such thing as a little white lie. Something is either true or it is a deception.

As long as a person can lie and feel comfortable about it or even justify it, it will be impossible to resist temptation, and the sins that violate the commitment between us and God, and particularly that between husbands and wives, will continue to flourish.

Some point to instances in Scripture in which men and women we would consider heroes told lies. Since the Bible doesn't specifically condemn such individuals, modern readers sometimes assume that under certain circumstances God condones lying. Rahab, the prostitute who lived in Jericho, is a case in point. She told a lie to protect the two spies that came to her house (Joshua 2:4). Thus some interpret this to mean that the Bible accepts situation ethics, in which if you lie to save a life, it is God's will.

If that were true, then it would, in effect, be playing the Ten Commandments against each other. A woman could be a prostitute to earn money to send the gospel to the unsaved, or a man could rob a bank to provide financial resources for the needy.

The Scriptures are scathingly honest. They tell the life stories of men and women who later became heroes for the Lord. But just because they served God doesn't mean that everything they did along the way was to His glory or is a model for the Christian life.

I say this not to diminish any Bible character. My point is that we will continue in our sins and perish in our sins unless we become perfectly honest with God, with ourselves, and with others. John 8:32 says: "And ye shall know the truth, and the truth shall make you free." The passage implies not only that there is an objective truth that is in Jesus Christ but that we ourselves must come to the place where we prefer the truth. Not only must we commit ourselves to hear the truth; we must dedicate ourselves to tell the truth. The Scriptures teach that the lost not only tell lies but also love to hear lies themselves (Rev. 22:15).

We live in a society that no longer regards truth as important and sees lying as definitely an option. But with God truth is everything, and lying is unacceptable. How does God feel about those who persist in telling lies? Proverbs 12:22: "Lying lips are abomination to the Lord: but they that deal truly are his delight." Proverbs 19:9: "A false witness shall not be unpunished, and he that speaketh lies shall perish." 1 Timothy 4:1, 2: "Now the Spirit speaketh expressly, that in the latter times some shall depart from the faith, giving heed to seducing spirits, and doctrines of devils; speaking lies in hypocrisy; having their conscience seared with a hot iron."

The Scriptures are clear. We don't have to read between the lines or study Greek or Hebrew to understand the Bible's position. If we prefer to hear lies and persist in telling them, we will not and cannot be saved.

Earlier I pointed out that lying may be the most serious of sins because it is the umbrella under which we justify everything else we do. Lying is fatal to spiritual growth, because it blocks us from receiving the truth, and only truth can set us free from sin. "Ye shall know the truth, and the truth shall set you free" (John 8:32). To put it simply, we cannot gain victory over any sin until we have gotten victory over telling lies.

Proverbs 28:13 says it plainly: "He that covereth his sins shall not prosper: but whoso confesseth and forsaketh them shall have mercy." How could it be more clear? As long as we persist in trying to hide our sins from others and from ourselves we will not repent, and if we will not repent, God cannot forgive or show mercy.

Some years ago I had an experience I will never forget. I had decided to preach a sermon on lying. Up until that moment I had never dealt with the subject in an organized manner.

But I couldn't think of how to present the subject in a way that people hadn't already heard before. I happened to be traveling at the time, and on that particular morning I sat waiting in my motel room for my colleagues to come for me. I decided that I would spend the time trying to get some thoughts together for the sermon.

Since I didn't have a notebook, I found some small pieces of paper in the room that didn't have anything printed on the backs. Just as I began to jot down some thoughts someone knocked at the door of the room. When I called out, "Come in," a hotel maid who appeared to be in her late 20s or early 30s entered the room.

When she saw me at the table she said, "Excuse me; I'll come back later."

"Don't mind me," I replied. "You may go ahead with your work."

She went into the bathroom to take out the towels. In a minute or two she had finished in the bathroom and was beginning to change the sheets on the bed. Suddenly I decided I would ask her what she thought of lying. "I am a minister," I explained, "and I am preparing a sermon on lying. May I ask you a question?" Without waiting for her to reply I continued, "When is it all right to lie?"

She stopped what she was doing, looked over at me, and said, "Never!"

What did I expect? How could she say anything else to a minister who was preparing a sermon on lying? Then she continued, "But I used to lie when I figured that if I didn't things might not turn out well for me."

I begin to take notes, then asked, "You said that you used to lie. What made you to stop?"

"I stopped lying when I found out how God feels about it," she replied. "Do you know why we lie? We lie because we don't trust God." A light went on in my mind. She was right. Sometimes when we struggle with problems we may feel that being truthful will get us into bigger difficulties, and so we try to cover up. Then the maid continued, "But we don't have to worry, because greater is He that is in us than he that is in the world."

I could hardly believe what I was hearing! For a moment I even wondered if she really was a hotel maid or whether she might possibly be an angel God had sent to help me understand something I had not contemplated before.

But she wasn't through yet. As she continued to make the bed she concluded, "The alcoholic says that if he doesn't have booze, he can't make it. The drug addict says that if he doesn't have drugs, he can't make it. I want my life to be such that if I don't have Jesus, I won't be able to make it."

I thank God that He allowed me to meet this woman who made the bed and straightened the room that day. I now had what I needed for a sermon and will never forget what she told me.

As we approach the end of time it is vital that we submit our hearts and lives completely to all that the Holy Spirit wants to do not only for us but in us (Phil. 2:13). Yet He will not be able to accomplish anything unless we are perfectly honest with Him, with ourselves, and with others.

Our society no longer bases itself on truth; neither does it regard truth as essential. We find ourselves bombarded with so many lies that we are losing the ability to recognize them. Worse still, we are beginning to prefer hearing lies to hearing the truth. As the maid in the motel said, many hide behind lies when they fear that telling the truth would get them into trouble.

She was right. We do not yet trust God the way we should, the way we must, if He is to transform us (Heb. 13:21; Phil. 1:6).

Let us be truthful with ourselves and with God and own up to our sins and mistakes. You may fear that if you squarely face the truth about yourself, it will be more than you can bear. But as the maid said, we must trust God. Let us not be afraid to face the reality about ourselves. When we do, only then will we be able to understand and experience the power in God's promise that if we confess our sins, He will forgive us and cleanse us from all unrighteousness (1 John 1:9). But how can He forgive our sins unless we confess them? How can He cleanse us from unrighteousness unless we admit that we have no excuse for the things that we do contrary to His will?

## What Is Important to Know

1. Lying is what we do when we don't want to face reality.

2. Unless we face reality, we will not admit that we are doing wrong.

3. Unless we admit doing wrong, we will simply continue to do it.

4. Lying is the "cover" sin that makes it possible for us to justify the other sins we commit, and therefore it blocks the work that the Holy Spirit is trying to do in our lives.

## Personal Application

1. The Bible speaks of those who love to hear lies. What times would we prefer to hear lies rather than the truth?

2. You have heard the expressions "Tell it like it is" and "Let the chips fall where they may." We also say sometimes that the truth hurts. Does that mean we should purposely use truth to injure others? A hint: Although Jesus never told a lie, how did He handle the truth?

---

### Prayer

Our Father in heaven, You sent Jesus to live here among us, and He told us He is the way, the truth, and the life because He trusted in You. He always made it a practice to tell the truth, even when things were not going to turn out right for Him.

Lord, forgive us for not trusting You. When we lie we take matters into our own hands, and worse still, when we habitually lie to others we begin to lie to You and to ourselves. This keeps us from admitting our sins and letting the Holy Spirit transform our lives.

Please make us sensitive and careful to be truthful with You, with ourselves, and with others. As spiritual darkness covers the earth, may Your truth be a lamp to light our way. We pray this in the name of Him who is the way, the truth, and the life. Amen.

# *Expect to Think Differently*

Y ou will remember that at the end of chapter 3 we said we were going to look at two things that work against repentance and even make it impossible. In the last chapter we observed that lying keeps us from repenting. In this chapter we will discover the other thing that blocks repentance.

It may sound strange, but many people who call themselves Christians don't believe some of the things Jesus taught. They especially have difficulty with Matthew 23:12, which states that those who humble themselves will be exalted, and verse 11, in which He calls on us to be servants.

In this chapter we will go head-to-head with these teachings of our Lord. These passages and many others that we could put alongside them amount to just the opposite of what most people expect of how we should relate to others. We generally don't have trouble with the idea that we ought to love each other, but from a practical point of view we have an enormous problem with the concept of humility.

In some areas of the world servants are still very much a part of the culture. I have lived where many people had servants, and sometimes even the servants had servants. Certain cultures have a class of society called the "servant class." Persons from this class may become educated and even have money, but others will always regard them as belonging to the servant class.

Christ's teaching of what it means to be a servant comes into sharp focus in an incident related in John 13:4, 5. During the Last Supper Jesus got up from the table, laid aside His garments, took a towel, and girded Himself. And after that He poured water into a basin and began to wash the disciples' feet and to wipe them with the towel.

So dramatic was the impact of what He was doing that when He came to Peter, the disciple basically said, "Don't touch me. Don't even think about it!"

In other cultures the feet have special significance. When I visited Thailand for the first time I received an instruction sheet that listed the cultural norms of the country. One of the rules, believe it or not, had to do with feet.

It stated that when sitting on a platform one should never point their feet at anyone. To do so would be considered a serious insult.

Some years later the significance of that custom came home to me in a startling way. I read an account in the newspaper that illustrated how serious this matter is in that part of the world, even though the incident took place in Los Angeles, California. The article told of a murder that occurred outside a nightclub involving two men from Southeast Asia. One of the men was a patron of the club and the other a singer. The article explained that as the soloist performed that night, the patron sat with his feet inadvertently pointed toward the singer. Later that night when the club closed, the soloist followed the patron outside and shot him.

When I read that, I realized as never before the significance that feet have in the minds of so many in the world, and it made me understand even more what Peter meant when he said to the Lord, "Don't touch me. You will never wash my feet." When Jesus knelt to wash the disciples' feet, it had an incredible cultural impact.

The part of Southern Asia where I lived for a time had an expression of disdain, "I showed him my shoe." I was returning from town one day and had stopped at a filling station for gasoline when I heard a tremendous ruckus. Glancing in its direction, I saw a large crowd. As I watched I noticed two men fighting. A crowd pushed, shouted, and cursed. Suddenly several men in the crowd stepped in to mediate the fight. That produced more shouting and gesturing as each side tried to tell its point of view. Then I saw one of the arbitrators take a shoe and tap one of the fighters lightly on the shoulder. Obviously that humiliated the hapless man. The gesture seemed to satisfy the crowd, which quieted down and soon wandered away.

Back in the 1950s Nikita Khrushchev, at that time leader of the Soviet Union, visited the United Nations. Some may recall how he took off his shoe during a speech by one of the ambassadors and began to pound it on the desk. People from Western cultures saw this and thought he was crazy and uncivilized. But millions around the world understood exactly what he was trying to convey—his disdain and lack of respect for what the speaker had to say.

As Jesus washed the feet of those disciples, He was making Himself about as low as anyone could get according to society's norms. When He was through washing the disciples' feet, He said, "I have given you an example, that ye should do as I have done to you" (John 13:15). Although we have adopted foot washing as a ritual, we may be missing the point of it all. Jesus was saying that He expects us to relate to each other with a spirit of complete humility. That is what He meant when He said, "He that is greatest among you shall be your servant" (Matt. 23:11). Here is where we face a dilemma, because we know very few people who have become great by being servants, and we have a hard time believing what Jesus said.

Contemporary society tells us to watch out for ourselves first. Some even suggest we get in front of a mirror, look ourselves in the eye, and say, "I love me!" The message is that we must stick up for our rights and not let people walk on us. We live in a dog-eat-dog society. What Jesus said may be true in theory, but surely not in practice.

In my own heart I feel the dilemma. I hear, as it were, Jesus say, "He that is greatest among you, let him be your servant," yet everywhere I look it seems as though those who get ahead put themselves first. The world tells us that we should watch out for number one, while Jesus says we should put others first. What should we expect?

As we assemble the puzzle pieces of the Christian life and find a piece like this one which doesn't seem to fit, we must go back to the big picture. Remember, at the beginning of this book we learned that successful Christian living depends upon our accepting God's expectations for us. He has made it plain in His Word that His plan for us is that we be like Jesus. It means that humility in the Christian walk is not an option. The issue is not Will we or will we not be humble? but How, by God's grace, will we accomplish it?

Jesus gives us a practical illustration of how this is done. He said we shouldn't do just what others tell us, we need to do even more. You are familiar with the text that declares that if someone makes you carry something a mile, do one better and go two. It refers to the fact that Roman soldiers could legally force the Jewish people to carry any kind of burden for them for one mile (Matt. 5:41).

Putting this into today's perspective, if you do only what your employer tells you, it is possible to become indifferent and even resentful. Many times I have talked with people who said, "I quit my job today. I'm not going to let those guys tell me what to do all the time." Human nature resents being told what to do. That's why Jesus said we shouldn't do just what we're told—rather, He calls on us to exceed what is expected of us. Thus when someone asks you to go a mile, make it two. Or if someone requests your jacket, hand them your overcoat as well. Believe it or not, here is the secret for making humility practical.

Watch how this can work at home. Let's suppose my wife asks

me to take out the garbage under the kitchen sink when I'm doing something else. Can't she see I'm busy? Doesn't she recognize that I'm trying to study? Nevertheless, I do what she asks, but under my breath I am mumbling all the while.

How can I change that? Here's the way to do it using the second-mile principle. The next time my wife requests that I take out the garbage, I think to myself that, as long as I am going to do it, I might as well empty the wastebaskets from the bathrooms and bedrooms at the same time. The minute I decide to more than asked, my whole perspective changes. Now I don't feel as though I'm being pushed around, that I have no choice except to do what I'm told. Instead I consider myself a partner. I am actually taking part in the decision-making process, and it makes both my wife and me happy. The point is—we demonstrate humility by exceeding expectations.

But what about people who exploit us? At times that may happen. People may take advantage of us. Sometimes it seems as if certain people wake up in the morning thinking to themselves, *I'm going to rip off someone today.* Scripture addresses that problem when it says, "Vengeance is mine; I will repay, saith the Lord" (Rom. 12:19). It even goes a step further and promises a blessing for those who find themselves wronged and exploited by others. Jesus says: "Blessed are ye, when men shall revile you, and persecute you, and shall say all manner of evil against you falsely, for my sake. Rejoice, and be exceeding glad: great is your reward in heaven" (Matt. 5:11, 12).

Two people did some scuba diving in Florida. They planned to explore an underground river. One of the divers was deep in an underwater cave when suddenly he noticed that apparently his air bubbles were going down instead of up. You don't have to be a rocket scientist to know that air bubbles in the water don't fall, they rise. When he saw that, he knew that he had become disoriented. His senses tried to convince him his air bubbles were descending, but his reason said that they had to be rising.

He knew he had to get to the surface or die. But which way was up? He must decide now. If he followed the bubbles, his instincts warned him that he would be going to his death, because his confused physical senses indicated that he would be diving deeper. Yet he knew in his mind that bubbles don't go down. If he were going to save his life, he would have to follow the bubbles no matter how he felt. And so he swam along with his bubbles apparently down, down, down (according to his feelings), until at last he reached the surface.

We read in the Scriptures that those who exalt themselves shall be abased, and those who humble themselves shall be exalted, and that the greatest among people is the servant. Although we know that must be the way it is because Jesus said so, it jolts our human nature. Experience has taught us that we must look out for ourselves. It feels to us as though we have to defend our rights, that if we don't push others aside, we will never get ahead. Are we to believe what we see and feel—or Scripture?

Oh, yes, people may revile and persecute us. Someone may walk on us. What will we do? How will we react? I want to respond like Jesus. He was King of kings and Lord of lords, yet He girded Himself and washed feet.

Often I feel my pride and selfishness fighting for dominance, but in the kingdom of heaven, up is down. "Every one that exalteth himself shall be abased; and he that humbleth himself shall be exalted" (Luke 18:14). I can't solve all the problems this concept might bring into your life. But I can assure you that this is the way it is, and that each one of us in our own lives will have to come to grips with it, because the servant is not greater than the Master. Jesus humbled Himself, and so must we (Phil. 2:7, 8). He humbled Himself, not so that we wouldn't need to, but so that in spite of our pride and selfishness we can, through the Holy Spirit, be like Him.

I said at the beginning of this chapter that we would discover something else that makes repentance impossible. It is pride and selfishness. We will touch again on this issue in chapter 16, "Expect to Pray Better."

## What Is Important to Know

1. Christians grow up by growing down.

2. Accepting Jesus' call to be a servant to others in the face of society's insistence that we look out for ourselves first may well be one of the greatest acts of faith that God summons us to do.

3. As society becomes more and more obsessed with selfishness, the committed Christian will find it increasingly difficult to fit in.

4. We will soon experience to the full extent what it means to walk by faith and not by sight.

## Personal Application

1. In what practical ways would your lifestyle need to change in order to incorporate the principle of humility mandated by our Lord?

2. How does a person following the spirit of humility that Christ modeled relate to someone trying to take advantage of them?

## Prayer

Dear Father, it is more than we can comprehend! You tell us to be humble, and yet everything around us says Don't be so foolish. Although You tell us that if we will humble ourselves we will be exalted, experience declares that life is not that way at all.

Thank You for sending your Son to show us what it looks like to be the lowest of all. Knowing that we must believe Him, we recognize that pride and selfishness make repentance impossible, yet unless we repent we cannot be saved. O God, do whatever it takes for us to be like Jesus. You promised that before this is over we will be like Him. In our own strength we can't do it. Like the blind and the lame that Jesus healed of their infirmities, so heal us of our pride and selfishness. Teach us how to serve You and each other so that Jesus will be glorified in our lives. Amen.

# Expect to Develop a New Conscience

In 1984 an Avianca Airlines jet crashed. One of the first things accident investigators do is try to locate the black box cockpit recorder. In this case they made an eerie discovery. The recorder revealed that several minutes before the crash a computer-synthesized voice from the plane's automatic warning system repeatedly told the flight crew in English, "Pull up, pull up."

The pilot must have thought the system was malfunctioning. The black box recorder captured the pilot telling the device to shut up; then he apparently switched the system off. Minutes later the plane plowed into the side of a mountain. Everyone on board died. It is a tragic story, yet it is a perfect parable of the way people today are treating the warning messages of their consciences.

Many assume that guilt causes our difficulties. As a result we will do whatever it takes to avoid a guilt trip. However, contrary to popular thinking, guilt does not create our most severe problems. It cannot be the culprit, because guilt is not a cause but rather an effect. Guilt is something that the conscience detects. Therefore, if we are going to address what to do about guilt, we must first understand what the conscience is and what role it plays in the Christian life. If our perception of guilt is not accurate and we treat it as a cause rather than as an effect, we could wake up one day to discover that the steps we took to remedy guilt in fact made it impossible for us to be free from what was creating the trouble in the first place.

God planned that the conscience should warn us of the moral implications of what we do or plan to do (Isa. 30:21). He designed the conscience to react to lawlessness and irresponsibility. It registers guilt, shame, and even fear of punishment. While society may see the conscience as a defect that robs people of their self-esteem, it is simply not true. The conscience doesn't create guilt (Isa. 59:2)—it detects it. God placed the conscience into the very fiber of the human soul to be an automatic warning system that tells us "Pull up, pull up" before we crash and burn. When we understand what the conscience is for, we can appreciate that it is one of the greatest gifts God has given us.

The conscience is that part of us that separates us from the rest of God's creation on our planet. It is the ability God has given us to know right and wrong. Conscience is that part of humanity that reflects the image of God (Gen. 1:26). Animals don't have a conscience. When snakes bite or lions kill, they are not violating their conscience. Nor do they have the ability to make moral self-evaluations on the level that human beings do.

The conscience is a human faculty. Even though sometimes it may not seem like it, everybody has one. "For when the Gentiles, which have not the law, do by nature the things contained in the law, these, having not the law, are a law unto themselves: which shew the work of the law written in their hearts, their conscience also bearing witness, and their thoughts the mean while accusing or else excusing one another" (Rom. 2:14, 15).

Though a person is born with the faculty of conscience, it is important that we understand it is neither God's voice nor His law. The conscience simply judges our actions and thoughts in the light of the highest standard we happen to understand at the time.

The conscience is not infallible, because it can be tainted. The role of the conscience is not to teach moral and ethical ideals. Nor can the conscience decide by itself what is right and wrong. It only reminds us what is right and wrong according to the way we have programmed it. Inasmuch as tradition and environment as well as truth can shape our conscience, it may or may not reflect biblical truth.

The conscience may be sensitized to things that are not biblical issues. For that matter, at the other extreme it may be totally unresponsive to things that are clearly a moral issue. It is even possible to have a conscience that has no foundation in the Word of God. When this happens, it will spin its wheels a lot but will not take us anywhere. For this reason a strong, regular input of Scripture is necessary to strengthen a weak conscience. It will also help to stabilize one that disturbs us for nonbiblical reasons. If the conscience is going to function as it is supposed to, it must be programmed and continually updated by the Word of God.

Sometimes we hear the advice "Just let your conscience be your guide." That is not a safe criterion because it takes for granted that a person has a sensitive, developed conscience based on the Word of God and that nothing has blunted it or rendered it inoperative. Like a fine instrument, our consciences must be well calibrated with the Word of God. Some people have consciences so corrupted that they can commit terrible crimes and afterward say that their conscience never bothered them. The Word of God in effect must be the operating system of the conscience. Psalm 119:11 says it best: "Thy word have I hid in mine heart, that I might not sin against thee."

The conscience of many people is becoming more and more unreliable, because they base their sense of right and wrong on consensus. That is, they let society set their moral standards. We have come to a time in which we cannot permit conscience to be our final criterion. The Word of God must be our guide, and in every situation we must subject our conscience to its standard.

The point is that the conscience functions like a window, not like a lightbulb. It lets light into the soul, but does not produce its own illumination. Therefore the amount of pure light we let in and how clean we keep the windows will determine the effectiveness of our conscience.

Contrary to what the contemporary culture may be claiming, God has not given the conscience to censure but to protect. It is wrong actions that condemn us. God has put the conscience there to alert us and to tell us when we have swerved off the moral road.

It is important to understand that it is possible to dull the conscience or even to make it inoperable (Titus 1:15; Eph. 4:19). If we resist the voice of conscience or keep it uninformed or misinformed, it will cease to work or even begin to malfunction.

For some years my work took me to Africa. It was there that I witnessed the scourge of leprosy for the first time. Leprosy is a disease that makes it impossible for the person affected to feel pain. I saw men and women without feet and hands. It had been my understanding that the disease destroys the extremities. But that is not so. The disease simply takes away the sensation of pain, and without pain its victims cannot tell when they are injuring their hands and feet. It helped me understand how the conscience is the moral organ of pain. A person who ignores their conscience or seeks to do away with it will sooner or later end up badly disfigured morally and eventually may lose their soul.

I had often wondered why people raised in a Christian environment and who then leave it could end up worse than those who had lived in the world all their lives. People with a primitive or undeveloped conscience but who are responsive to it will often not be nearly as bad as people who have turned their back on their conscience and, in the words of Scripture, "crucify . . . the Son of God afresh" (Heb. 6:6).

It is more serious to have known truth and rejected it than not to have known it at all. The apostle Paul speaks of this phenomenon in 1 Timothy 4:1, 2: "Now the Spirit speaketh expressly, that in the latter times some shall depart from the faith, giving heed to seducing spirits, and doctrines of devils; speaking lies in hypocrisy; having their conscience seared with a hot iron."

A person who has defiled or blunted their conscience will end up being like a ship without a compass. The warning signals that previously made them feel guilty are gone, but the danger remains. Without a way to detect moral problems, they are in greater danger than ever.

I had an experience that helped me understand the importance of a sensitive conscience. Some years ago I owned a 1985 Ford LTD station wagon. On the dashboard the car had what many call "idiot lights," although I am sure the manufacturer didn't refer to them by that term. Idiot lights are different than gauges. An oil gauge will show you what your oil pressure is as you drive along. An idiot light doesn't come on until the engine is out of oil, and by then it is probably too late. Two times I burned the head on my engine because the light flashed on after the damage had already taken place. The second time it happened I paid to have gauges installed that constantly monitored the condition of the engine (you could say I was an idiot not to have put the gauges in the first time!).

The gauges on a car are there to tell us what the condition of the motor is and to help us prevent problems. When problems do erupt, the gauge indicates that we should stop and do something about it. In the same way God intended our conscience to alert us when we have wandered into dangerous territory in our lives. I suspect that much of the pain we suffer in our lives results from the fact that we have not paid attention to the signals that we have received from our conscience, or that our conscience is not calibrated by the Word of God and has been blunted.

Living in a "take away the pain" society, we tend to be much more interested in alleviating symptoms than in discovering their causes. I want my conscience to be programmed by the Word of

God, and I need it to be highly sensitive. Instead of having my conscience like a filter so loose that a "basketball" could easily get through, I desire one that is such a fine filter it will immediately detect even a grain of sand that is not in harmony with the will of God for my life.

Some might interpret this to mean that I am always on a guilt trip. Not really. Whether we are on a guilt trip or not depends on what we do about it. When the oil gauge on my car indicates that the pressure is low, whether or not I then burn up my engine depends not on the gauge but on what I choose to do about it. I can ignore the gauge or even disable it, but the problem is still there and will get worse until I deal with it.

The gospel of Jesus is made for the engine problems that come into our lives. My favorite text is the one that says that if we confess our sins, He will not only forgive them but fix our problem—that is, to cleanse us from all unrighteousness (1 John 1:9).

## What Is Important to Know

1. A functioning, sensitized conscience is a gift from God.

2. The conscience is not God's voice, but a human faculty that we must program.

3. We cannot trust our conscience unless we are sure that we are constantly keeping it calibrated by the Word of God.

4. Guilt indicates that the conscience is functioning. Instead of a cause it is an effect (we will study guilt further in the next chapter).

## Personal Application

1. How do the words of Jesus that the one who is faithful in little things is also faithful in big ones (Luke 16:10) apply to the health and well-being of our conscience?

2. If it is possible to have a "seared" conscience, what may cause a conscience to register "off the wall"?

### Prayer

Lord, we are embarrassed and ashamed that we tend to resent the very thing You have given us to protect us and tell us when we are off track. Thank You that You have provided us with a conscience that can indicate our nearness to Your will. We want to have a healthy, sensitive conscience.

We pray that Your Holy Spirit will remind us to keep our conscience calibrated with Your Word. And we are thankful that the gospel has everything we need to pull us out of the ditch of sin we so easily drive into.

Also we are thankful that You don't hold our past against us, and that even when we keep making mistakes because of our carelessness and indifference, You are always waiting to set our feet on solid ground again. Thank You that You are merciful, gracious, long-suffering, and full of goodness. Amen.

# Expect to Feel Guilty

In the previous chapter we learned that the conscience produces the phenomenon we speak of as guilt. A person who doesn't feel guilt from time to time should worry, because it indicates the conscience has become dysfunctional. Society, though, is highly sensitive to guilt and tells us we should not feel guilty. It is not unusual to hear someone say "Don't try to lay a guilt trip on me."

But the purpose of Scripture is to do just that. It is supposed to make us sense guilt. Notice 2 Timothy 3:16: "All scripture is given by inspiration of God, and is profitable for doctrine, for reproof, for correction, for instruction in righteousness." Reproof and correction may very well result in feelings of guilt.

I once heard a pastor comment in his sermon that one thing he would not do was make his congregation feel guilty. He said some people enjoy wallowing in guilt, but he was not into that. Neither am I. But when the Bible is the basis for the preaching, guilt is often the result. The purpose of preaching is to open the Word of God and let it speak for itself. It is possible for a person to read the Bible alone even on a desert island and come under the conviction that he or she is a sinner in the eyes of God.

My computer has a program called Norton Utilities. I run it often, since it checks out the hard disk. If it detects a problem, it will ask me if I want it to remedy it. When I hit the return key, it will deal with the problem and then report "Fixed."

The procedure is important for the health and well-being of the computer's hard disk. The program doesn't create disk problems—it performs a diagnosis and then fixes the problems. However, to solve the problem, I have to run the program. When the window informs me it has detected a problem, I don't run screaming from the room, neither do I get a hammer and smash the screen of the computer. But you may be sure I do not ignore the warning. When the Word of God reproves us and corrects us it is not putting us down—it is doing just the opposite. It is picking us up and giving us an opportunity to get back on track.

Jesus promised He would send the Holy Spirit, whose first task would be to convict us of sin (John 16:7, 8). Correction is necessary because we must realize we are wrong before we can feel any need to change. The law of motion is that an object will continue moving in the direction it is headed until it meets an outside force that changes its direction. Guilt is the feeling that something has gone wrong. The prodigal son had to feel guilty before he decided to return home (Luke 15:18).

The truth is that when we make a mistake we are guilty and we should feel guilty. But unless we admit our guilt and recognize it as a symptom that something is wrong, we will probably continue in the direction we were already headed.

One time I planned to attend a revival meeting being conducted in one of Florida's state prison facilities. It meant I would need to drive about 100 miles from where I live in Orlando. I gave myself plenty of time to get there, but for some unknown reason I decided to take a state road rather than the turnpike. I thought the state road went directly to the city of my destination.

After I drove more than 100 miles I began to wonder when I

would arrive. I continued another 50 miles and still had not reached the city. Finally I stopped at a convenience store and asked how much farther down the road I would I have to go to reach such-and-such a city. They politely informed me I was headed not toward my destination but toward Miami. I was on the wrong road and would have arrived in Miami had I not begun to feel "guilty" about why I had not yet reached my destination. Something was wrong with the direction in which I was headed, and I could do nothing about it until I admitted my error.

When we get the big picture we can see that guilt is a prerequisite to repentance. Scripture shows us our guilt so that the Holy Spirit can call us to repentance (John 16:8). Our society should be concerned about sin, but instead of repenting it is trying to rid itself of guilt, the result of sin.

If the biblical authors had lived in our day, they would not have been able to write the way they did. It would not have been politically correct. I have found many biblical confessions that do not match our present mind-set.

For instance, David declared: "Have mercy upon me, O God, according to thy loving kindness: according unto the multitude of thy tender mercies blot out my transgressions. Wash me thoroughly from mine iniquity, and cleanse me from my sin. For I acknowledge my transgressions: and my sin is ever before me. Against thee, thee only, have I sinned, and done this evil in thy sight: that thou mightiest be justified when thou speakest, and be clear when thou judgest. Behold, I was shapen in iniquity; and in sin did my mother conceive me" (Ps. 51:1-5).

Today he would have phrased it, "Lord, I messed up with that Bathsheba/Uriah thing. Sorry about that."

The prophet Daniel wrote in Daniel 9:5, 6: "We have sinned, and have committed iniquity, and have done wickedly, and have rebelled, even by departing from thy precepts and from thy judgments: neither have we hearkened unto thy servants the prophets, which spake in thy name to our kings, our princes, and our fathers, and to all the people of the land."

Why did he put himself down like that? Today he might have said: "Our parents made mistakes; we've made mistakes; but could You lighten up?"

Peter showed what a poor self-image he had. He fell down at Jesus' feet saying, "Depart from me; for I am a sinful man, O Lord" (Luke 5:8).

Some modern Peters might have protested, "Lord, could You give me some space? You're making me feel bad about myself."

Paul in Romans 7 held back nothing. He did not excuse himself by whining, "I am having some internal conflicts, but I'm sure these feelings of desperation are excessive."

The present trend to do away with guilt only makes things worse. But our lives are not going to be different until we address what is causing our guilt. If we seek to do away with guilt, we are only institutionalizing our sins and mistakes.

Scripture is clear that Jesus didn't come to condemn us. John 3:17 states: "For God sent not his Son into the world to condemn the world; but that the world through him might be saved." In another place John reports: "And Jesus said unto her, Neither do I condemn thee: go, and sin no more" (John 8:11). Though Jesus didn't come to condemn the sinner, He definitely sought to convict the sinner of his or her condition, and a convicted sinner will have a sense of guilt.

The Bible identifies two kinds of guilt. "Godly sorrow" produces a repentance that leads to salvation, but a "sorrow of the world" results in death (2 Cor. 7:10).

The two kinds of guilt differ in several ways.

1. Worldly guilt causes us to concentrate on ourselves, but godly guilt leads us to focus on the person we have offended. For example, if I am late for a meeting with someone, worldly sorrow dwells on how bad I feel about being tardy, but godly sorrow re-

minds me how my friend feels as he or she waits for me. In other words, worldly sorrow is self-centered, while godly sorrow thinks of the other person.

2. Worldly guilt obsesses on what we have done in the past. Godly guilt directs us to what we can do in the present to correct the problem we caused. While worldly sorrow keeps us focused on the sin, godly sorrow prompts us to take corrective action right now. Worldly sorrow lives in the past, godly sorrow in the here and now.

3. Any corrective action that emerges from worldly guilt stems only from a desire to stop feeling bad. But godly guilt prompts us to help the person whom we have wronged. The actions of godly guilt actually promote personal growth and focus on doing God's will.

4. Worldly sorrow will often result in temporary change, but rebellion may surface later on. Godly sorrow produces a true ongoing change.

The Bible does not worry how guilty we may or may not feel. It is instead concerned about the fact that we are actually guilty. The move these days to do away with guilt without dealing with what causes it can nullify the plan of salvation. Guilt leads to repentance, and repentance is the handle by which the forgiveness of God lifts us out of the pit of sin that we have fallen into. The issue we face is not who is a sinner and who isn't, but rather, inasmuch as we are all sinners, what we are going to do about it. I don't want my conscience to give me a green light until I have dealt with whatever activated the guilt.

It is as important for me to feel guilty when I do something wrong as it is for my finger to hurt when I touch a hot iron. Just as pain in the finger indicates danger, so guilt is God's way of alerting us to something that is not right. As we grow in grace and spiritual knowledge, guilt tells us when we have missed the mark. Do you feel guilty now and then? Thank God for it. It means you are alive and well. And we don't have to worry—God's grace is bigger than our guilt. If we confess our sins, He will take care of the rest (1 John 1:9).

Of course, we must be aware that there is also such a thing as toxic guilt. If conscience is the gauge God has given to tell us when something is wrong, then, as all gauges may do, it may go bad once in a while. Like a computer our conscience can "crash," and in certain instances we will need to "reboot" (restart) it.

Sometimes when the conscience does not reflect the Word of God or when we detect guilt in the conscience but do not deal with it, the guilt itself can become a problem. Toxic guilt can be a result of not following through on the call to repent, or it may even be a refusal to accept the fact that when we confess our sins God does forgive us.

It is important we understand that while God calls us to repent and accept His forgiveness, that forgiveness does not erase the fact that we will have to live with the results of what we have done. Those who say they believe God has forgiven them but still have not been able to forgive themselves may really mean that they are having a hard time accepting the consequences of what they have done. While the forgiveness of God serves to take away our guilt, we will usually have to live with the results of our sins and mistakes until Jesus returns. To put it in plain language, we may expect that while the gospel will take away the pain, we may always carry the scars (Gal. 6:7).

In conclusion, I am glad my conscience is alive and well and that it produces guilt in me when I need it. When dealt with promptly, guilt tells us when we drift off the road and lets us take corrective action before we actually hit something and cause permanent damage to our life. If we arrive at the place where we can value guilt and heed its warnings, we may not hurt ourselves as much as we have in the past.

---

## What Is Important to Know

1. A Christian may expect to feel guilty. We should not feel guilty about feeling guilty!

2. We should generally regard guilt as a result and not as a cause.

The Christian seeks to identify its root cause and accepts God's gift of repentance and forgiveness.

3. Guilt comes in two forms: "godly" and "worldly." Godly sorrow brings improvement and growth in the Christian life, while worldly sorrow tends to be superficial and blocks the gospel from addressing the real cause of the problem.

4. "Toxic guilt" can creep into our lives. Keeping the conscience educated by the Word of God and following through with repentance will keep guilt washed away and minimize the possibility of a warped conscience.

5. A clear conscience does not mean that we will avoid scars from our past. We may have to carry them until Jesus returns and makes all things new.

---

## Personal Application

1. Why is confessing to each other and asking for forgiveness for wrongs that we have committed important in being free from guilt?

2. What are some of the scars that you may have to carry as the result of past sins? Is there still any pain associated with these scars? What may it signify?

---

## Prayer

Dear Lord, while all around us things seem to be caving in, we are glad You have given us Your Word so we will not loose our way. Some try to convince us that we should not feel guilty. As You have endowed us with the sense of pain to protect our bodies, so You have given us the sense of guilt to protect our souls. Forgive us for sometimes taking an aspirin approach to what the Holy Spirit is trying to do in our lives. Too often we want the pain to go away without knowing what is causing it.

Lord, we recognize that our guilt can make us feel hopeless unless we believe what You have promised—that if we will admit we are wrong, You will forgive us and do everything necessary to get us back on the right road. We also recognize that Your forgiveness takes away pain but not scars. Give us the grace to bear the consequences of our past actions. We look forward to the time in which You will make all things new. Amen.

# Expect to Overcome Temptation–1

Once I heard a story about a missionary who lived in Africa when most travel still took place on foot. He always carried a high-powered rifle just in case he should happen to meet a dangerous animal along the way. Although he had carried his rifle for years, he had had no occasion to use it.

On this particular day, so the story goes, he was walking along a path in the bush (what they call the wild countryside in Africa). Tall elephant grass lined both sides of the path. As he rounded a bend in the trail he came face-to-face with a human-eating lion.

The instant he spotted the lion, the lion saw him. The missionary immediately, almost instinctively, brought the rifle up to his shoulder. In that same instant the lion crouched down to spring. As the missionary pulled the trigger the lion jumped. The shot missed the lion, but fortunately the lion went over the missionary. In the moment of confusion that followed. the man dodged through the tall grass and ran back to the mission station.

When he reached home his knees were knocking together, his face was flushed, and he was sweating profusely. "I have been a fool," he said to himself. "All these years I have been carrying this big hunting rifle, but because I haven't been practicing, I can't hit the side of a barn. If the lion hadn't misjudged the distance to me, I would be dead."

So then and there he decided not to let another day pass without setting up a target and practicing shooting until he could hit the bull's-eye.

The dawn of the next morning found him with a box of shells and his big rifle. He propped up a target just at the edge of the mission compound next to the jungle and began shooting at the target. After a few minutes he felt pretty good, because he was beginning to hit the bull's-eye now and then. As he continued to shoot he heard a strange sound coming from the tall grass not far from where he was practicing, but he kept on shooting. The strange commotion continued. At last he could resist his curiosity no longer. Laying his rifle aside, he walked to the grass, parted it, and saw the same lion practicing shorter jumps!

Of course, this story is only an illustration. But it does say something about the spiritual life. It reminds us of the Bible text that says that our enemy the devil rampages about like a roaring lion seeking its prey (1 Peter 5:8). The disciple calls us to eternal vigilance. We may expect that as long as we are alive here we will have to contend with the world, the flesh, and the devil. Therefore we must continually be on guard.

One common point of view suggests that we cannot overcome some temptations in our lives short of the return of Jesus. This philosophy is selective in which temptations it regards as overcomable and which it does not. Most people believe that we must resist and control drunkenness, drug addiction, rape, murder, spouse abuse, and child molestation. They are sins that society finds unacceptable. Yet some consider pride, anger, filthy imagination, and covetousness as irresistible temptations that must continue to ruin our lives and the lives of others.

Most of us do not consider ourselves to be dope addicts, drunkards, murderers, thieves, or rapists. But we struggle with selfishness, pride, temper, perverted imagination, bitterness, and covetousness. Some have tried countless times to break free, but it is easier said than done.

We are sinners, every one of us—even those who think they aren't (Rom. 3:23; 5:12). It's as natural for us to sin as it is for the sun to shine. However, there is a gate through which all sin must pass—the will. The will is the door through which all thought, imagination, and action must enter. In the case of a person who hasn't accepted Jesus, the door is basically stuck open. The traffic light is always green. The purpose of the gospel is to restore the power of choice, enabling us to open and close the door. When we accept Jesus as our Saviour, we get our power of choice back. Sin no longer has dominion over us (Rom. 6:14). And as we grow in grace, sinning increasingly becomes a matter of choice. We call this choice temptation (1 Cor. 10:13).

Many may find to their dismay that when they become a Christian they seem to face more temptation than ever. Part of this may be only a perception, because before we give our hearts to Jesus we do what comes naturally. We do not think in terms of a conflict between right and wrong, but simply tilt toward the wrong. It is when we have a moral conscience that we find ourselves tempted. Before that we are simply enticed (James 1:14). The question is not whether Christians will be tempted, but what they will do about it and how they will handle it. We can expect that as Christians we will encounter temptation. It goes with the turf. Jesus was tempted, and so will we be tempted (Matt. 4:1).

This chapter and the following one examine temptation and how as Christians we may deal with it. We must, of course, be aware that temptation is not sin but rather an invitation to sin. How we deal with it, then, is the difference between success and failure in our Christian walk.

The next two chapters will do two things: (1) they will lay down the principles we may use to resist temptation successfully, and (2) they will examine a specific temptation as an example to show how to apply these principles. You will notice that the example chosen is not a hypothetical one but represents a very real struggle in the lives of many Christians. Please remember that while we are referring to one temptation in particular, the principles apply to resisting all temptation. The example we will study is the temptation toward impure thoughts.

We live in an age of unprecedented immorality. Though the temptation of immorality has always existed, it has now infiltrated everywhere. Because of mass media the immorality in one sector of society can in a short time become worldwide in its impact. Impure sayings and impure songs sweep around the globe in a matter of weeks.

Christians have not been immune from all of this. It has taken a while, but impurity has made its inroads. More and more within the body of Christ have succumbed to extramarital sex. When we read that someone has robbed a bank we may have a hard time putting ourselves into the picture. The crime tempts few of us. But when we hear immoral stories we have no trouble identifying with them. All of us have bodies and biological and social drives.

The decision to overcome impure thoughts is a specific decision, yet if it is to be effective, it must be made within a framework of preexisting decisions and subsequently reinforced by other decisions.

I have divided the process of overcoming temptation into eight steps that I will cover in this and the following chapter. When we have these eight steps in place we will experience in an ever-increasing way the meaning of the promise that we are more than conquerors through Christ (Rom. 8:37) and also the promise that says Jesus is able to keep us from falling (Jude 24).

---

### *Step 1*

As we seek to overcome impure thoughts, we must keep in

mind that we are launching a war that we really want to win. The idea here must not be that we are trying to reduce the number of impure thoughts but that we want to get rid of them altogether. There is no such thing as an appropriate amount of moral impurity. Any amount of immorality is unacceptable. Daniel 1:8 gives the baseline for overcoming this and any other temptation when it says that Daniel determined in his heart that he would not defile himself.

One of our greatest challenges is to make up our mind. Many have tremendous problems in the area of moral impurity for the simple reason they have never really decided that they want to be pure. God cannot do something for us that we really do not want to have done. I suspect that many times we pray that God will do something in our lives not so much because we want it that way, but because someone else has convinced us that we need to change. And sometimes we will ask God to do things in our lives because we are afraid of what might happen if we don't seek His help.

We know God wants us to be pure, but no amount of prayer will help us until we decide we too have the same desire. Our prayer then should be "God, I want to be pure, not less impure but absolutely pure."

---

### Step 2

The next thing we must address is the matter of the imagination. In Psalm 51:2 David writes: "Wash me thoroughly from mine iniquity, and cleanse me from my sin." Impure acts begin in the imagination. No one falls into adultery—they walk into it. The mind is like a video player. Sexual impurity is not so much a matter of the organs and glands as it is a frame of mind. You may have heard people pray, or you may even have prayed yourself, that the Lord would take away sexual desire. But the procreative nature is something that God gave to the human race (Gen. 1:28). The problem is not in the way God has made us, but in the way we have allowed ourselves to become corrupted in our imagination. A morally corrupt lifestyle is the result of an immoral imagination. People who get into an immoral situation have first practiced it in their minds.

---

### Step 3

This step, a logical follow-up to the first two, requires that we be careful what we look at. The key to the control of the mind is the eye. Job 31:1 doesn't beat around the bush when the patriarch declares, "I made a covenant with mine eyes; why then should I think upon a maid?" To put this text in plain language, Job is saying that if he is going to be serious about the matter of impure thoughts, he is going to have stop looking at pretty girls. Temptation comes to us through the five senses, especially our eyes. Our culture surrounds us with pictures that easily suggest impure thoughts. Modern advertising often uses sensual elements to attract attention for its products. For example, advertisers may set up along the highway large billboards that feature suggestive pictures. People find themselves exposed to the billboards just because they happen to be traveling past them.

To review the process thus far I have determined that I want to overcome impure thoughts. I know that it is also what Jesus desires for me. So I have made a contract with my eyes that when I see something provocative, I will look the other way. At times such scenes may take me completely by surprise, but in most cases I know what to expect and can be prepared to resist the temptation. I have made it my custom while driving down the highway that when I see a suggestive billboard in the distance I simply do not to look at it. I have especially followed this practice when the road goes through areas containing "adult attractions." It would be foolish to look at suggestive signs and all the while be praying that God will take away the desire.

As you implement this step in your life you will find yourself encountering fewer and fewer situations that trigger impure thoughts in you.

## What Is Important to Know

1. Temptation is not sin, but an invitation to sin.

2. Christians will be aware of temptation in a way they weren't before they came to Christ.

3. Jesus was tempted, and we will be too.

4. We cannot ask God to do something in our lives that we really don't want done. Once we have decided we want Jesus to give us victory over temptation, as much as we possibly can we must take the steps necessary to reduce the opportunity for temptation to assail us.

## Personal Application

1. What kinds of things do you look at that increase the temptation to moral impurity?

2. Is moral impurity a problem only if a person is lusting for someone other than their spouse? Could moral impurity exist even in the context of marriage?

## Prayer

Father, we can see that in the past we been praying for You to do things in our lives that we have not really decided we wanted to happen. We also recognize that we have let our imaginations run wild and have even allowed our eyes to dwell on things that work against the very goals that we have been praying for.

Lord, we recognize that sometimes we have not been honest with You or with ourselves. We ask You to forgive us. Please don't give up on us! Even though we are unstable and vacillating, please continue to be patient with us, but don't let us off the hook. May the Holy Spirit convict us of our need of repentance and then, as You have promised, give us the grace and strength in that marvelous and mysterious way that only You can so that we may be truly free through Jesus, whom we love so much. Amen.

# *Expect to Overcome Temptation–2*

How often do we hear others talk about praying that the Holy Spirit will control their lives? The devil will definitely dictate our lives, but the Holy Spirit never will. He does, of course, change our hearts and lead us, but we will be disappointed if we expect the Spirit to control us.

The purpose of salvation is to break the stranglehold that sin has over us and return to us the power of choice. It means that a person who prays for the Spirit to lead will not be out of the decision loop but very much a part of it (Isa. 30:21). To submit to temptation or not is a choice we must make. Not only do we make the decision but we must follow through in implementing it. Also it is important for us to note that overcoming temptation cannot be a pick-and-choose approach if it is going to be successful. Though a puzzle may have many pieces, it is still one picture.

In this chapter we continue with some steps that when taken together will greatly reduce our temptations and effectively break their power over us. These steps draw their energy from the Holy Spirit and the love He has put in our hearts for Jesus Christ (2 Cor. 5:14).

---

### *Step 4*

As we resist temptation of any kind we need to be continually aware that the struggle is basically not physical but spiritual. Ephesians 6:12 explains: "For we wrestle not against flesh and blood, but against . . . spiritual wickedness in high places." Satan and his minions have a vested interest in contaminating our minds because it is in our minds that we resist temptation. Therefore he is going to do everything possible to trip us up and cause us to give in.

One evening I was about to catch a plane. I was in the airport walking down one of the corridors on the way to the gate when I passed a newsstand. A man with his back to me stood looking through a magazine with pictures in glossy color. A glance in his direction revealed that one of the pictures he was studying was definitely pornographic. As soon as I saw what it was, I turned my head away. It was not my fault I had seen it, nor was I the one who had opened the magazine. But I thought to myself, *Isn't it incredible how the devil continually hounds us in this respect. When we have made up our mind that we won't contaminate ourselves, that we don't want to defile our imagination, and have followed it up by making a covenant with our eyes— even then the devil will try every trick in the book to keep it from happening.*

You may be asking, So what is the difference? If you see something once, simply never think of it again. I wish it were that easy. The devil has a better memory than we do. He may wait until we are sitting in church, and then he will flash that picture at us again. Satan is the original dirty old man. He must have at least one of his imps assigned to us 24 hours a day, seven days a week. And he does everything he can to contaminate us and tempt us, because impurity and true spirituality are incompatible.

---

### *Step 5*

As we go through these various steps, please remember that although we are using a specific temptation as a example, the principles apply to any temptation. The next step is to remove from our surroundings anything that might contribute to our defeat and failure. Romans 13:14 states: "Make not provision for the flesh, to fulfil the lusts thereof." If you have been troubled with impure thoughts, then check around and you will probably discover your immediate environment full of suggestive elements. It might be the music you listen to, the magazines you read, or the television programs you watch.

I earned my way through college working on a plastering crew. The fellows I worked with couldn't seem to put two clean words together. Often I remember coming home from work after being with the guys all day and sitting down with the Bible so I could wash the things I had been hearing out of my mind. It gets to be pretty serious. But if we resist the devil, he will flee from us (James 4:7).

One of the elements that plays a large part in our thoughts is the music we listen to. If we are going to be serious about overcoming temptation, we must be careful about the kind of music we expose ourselves to. It is not my purpose to tell you what to listen to, but inasmuch as we are discussing how to overcome impure thoughts we need to remind ourselves that some music is sexually explicit and some is implicit.

Most Christians do not consciously choose impure music, but they are often not aware that even music without words creates a certain mood. If that were not true, then the dentist might play the theme from Alfred Hitchcock's *Psycho* in the waiting room. Another factor we often overlook is that although we may be listening to an instrumental rendition we may also be familiar with the lyrics, and as the music plays, our minds unconsciously repeat the words. Much of the easy listening music is about disappointed love, lust, and passion. Suffice it to say, if we are serious about getting victory over temptation, we must factor in the kind of music we immerse ourselves in.

### Step 6

Any serious program to overcome temptation of any kind requires that we always keep in mind that when we have won one battle we will have still others to fight. Earlier we learned that Christians can expect temptations. They will come from both outside and inside us. When we give our hearts to Jesus, that's not the end of our troubles. But it does mean that though the fight is far from over, we can now begin to win.

So if you struggle with temptations in your life, it doesn't mean that you don't love Jesus or that He doesn't love you. It's part of the Christian life. But if the devil walks all over you and you lose more often than you win, it is probably because there is a short circuit in your relationship with Him someplace. Check it out, and you will soon discover what is wrong. You may even want to use the eight steps in these chapters as a checklist. Jesus said that He came to set captives free (Luke 4:18). He wants to liberate us from the things that are ruining our lives, breaking up our homes, and corrupting us so badly.

During one business trip to Miami I stayed in a large motel. I had prepared for bed and spent a little time reading the Bible. After that I prayed, got into bed, and turned off the light. The light was barely out when the phone rang.

Reaching over, I picked it up and said hello. A feminine voice instantly started talking suggestively. As soon as I realized what was happening I hung up. Instead of rolling over and going to sleep, I turned on the light, took the Bible, and had my worship all over again. If somebody splatters mud in our face, we wash it off, don't we? Whoever it was that had called had, as it were, thrown mud in my mind.

We may expect the fight against temptation to be a lifetime battle. It will go on and on, but the difference is that now we are becoming winners through Christ (Rom. 8:37).

## *Step 7*

Another practical and effective way of overcoming temptation is unfortunately not very popular in the contemporary culture. Proverbs 16:6 states that it is by the fear of the Lord that human beings depart from evil. Some are not comfortable with the idea of fearing God. Yet the text is true in the battle with temptation. Fear in the biblical sense invokes awe, respect, and loyalty. Not only can the fear of the Lord assist us in overcoming temptation, but believe it or not, so can the fear of each other. If we respect others, we will not violate our relationships with them or their trust in us..

When we lived in South America I worked with the Adventist Relief and Development Agency (ADRA). ADRA conducts many of its programs in cooperation with the Agency for International Development (USAID). ADRA had a large food distribution program for malnourished children in the country where I served. One summer USAID invited me and representatives of other voluntary agencies to attend a food warehousing seminar to convene in a city in Central America. We arrived at the seminar, and all registered at the same hotel. Shortly afterward I noticed to my surprise several of the delegates in the company of prostitutes. It became apparent to me that when the men were out of their own environment they did things they would not have dared to do at home. They were violating the trust others had in them and were not making themselves accountable to their associates.

Once a Christian worker stopped at a restaurant one Friday evening. Not only did the restaurant serve food but it offered music and dancing. A girl came over to his table, tapped him on the shoulder, and invited him to dance. Carelessly he got up and began to dance with her. There happened to be a former church member in the room who recognized him and called the church headquarters on Monday morning. Fortunately, things went no farther than the dance floor, but the incident damaged the worker's effectiveness.

This is why when I travel I like to stay with God's people. When I am with them, I know the angels are there and I'm in the right place. I appreciate being accountable. It makes it easier to resist temptation. By the fear of the Lord and our accountability to each other we can protect ourselves from temptation.

---

### Step 8

This step ensures victory every time you find yourself tempted to have an impure thought. Based on Romans 6, it offers the secret for overcoming any temptation. Verse 1 begins with a question: "What shall we say then? Shall we continue in sin, that grace may abound?" Then, to phrase it as we would today, the passage answers, "No way." "How shall we," it asks rhetorically, "that are dead to sin, live any longer therein?" And then it begins to unfold the secret. "Know ye not that so many of us as were baptized into Jesus Christ were baptized into His death? . . . Like as Christ was raised up from the dead by the glory of the Father, even so we also should walk in newness of life" (Rom. 6:1-6).

In two words, the secret to overcoming temptation is "Play dead"! When we find ourselves tempted with impure thoughts or to participate in any other sin that may come along, the way we can handle it is simply to say this little prayer (using the temptation to impure thoughts as an example): "How can I, who am dead to impurity, live any longer therein?" And that's the end of it, because dead people do not have impure thoughts.

Chapter 2 addressed the significance of the cross. This step affirms that we have died (that the old human being of sin has been crucified with Christ) and that we are now alive in Christ (having been born again). Try it; it works! However, don't be surprised if you face temptation five minutes later. But once you begin to respond using this model, through the power of the Holy Spirit you will notice that your ability to discern temptation and to resist will greatly improve (Rom. 8:11-14). By the way, it also works for the temptation to lose your temper or to criticize someone. People who are dead don't criticize their neighbor. Mothers who are dead don't scream at their children.

Some of us lose in the battle against temptation so often that we have begun to believe that we have no way out and that all we know how to do is damage control. It is time to take the offensive, to raise a shield against the temptation (Eph. 6:16).

Finally, I have saved the best for last. I won't classify what comes next as step 9; rather I see it as an upgrade of step 8. Of course, you must use it in conjunction with the other seven steps. Don't forget, resisting temptation is a process and each component is important. It will help you with temptations that up to now you may have found impossible to resist. You may have tried everything and nothing works—or at least not for long. What you are about to learn now will work every time. I must tell you that this response to temptation is a little more involved. It takes some organization, but once all the pieces are in place it is unbeatable.

This strategy has two parts. Before I tell you what they are I must first ask you a question. Do you have anyone in your life who has fallen away from the Lord or who needs to find Jesus? No matter where I have asked this question people always know someone. So the first thing we must do is identify this person in our mind. For the sake of the exercise I will use the name Aunt Mary. Now that we have identified a person who needs the Lord, we can proceed.

The second part in this strategy requires that we make a decision. We must decide that the next time we are tempted, the temptation itself will serve as a reminder to us to pray for Aunt Mary. You can imagine that if you were the devil and you had assigned one of your imps to harass someone, but now that harassment caused the person to begin to pray for someone else who needed the Lord, you would think twice about whether it was worth bothering the first individual. The last thing the devil wants is for us to intercede for the lost.

You can see at once why this method is so effective. It stops the temptation in its tracks, and it puts us on the offensive rather than on the defensive. While the prayer declaring we are dead to temptation is like putting up a shield, this second method not only erects a shield but actually fights back at a level that makes the temptation fail while advancing the kingdom of heaven through our intercessory prayer.

Deciding in advance what to do when temptation rears its head is essential. If we have made up our mind to resist temptation, then when it does surface we don't have to consider whether we want to resist or not. That has already been settled. It gives us full energy to cooperate with the Holy Spirit in becoming the overcomers that Jesus desires us to be and that we ourselves have decided we want to be (1 John 2:14).

---

### What Is Important to Know

1. It is natural and normal for the Christian to be tempted. We must determine in advance how to resist and overcome.

2. A healthy fear of God and our fellow human beings can act as a deterrent to temptation.

3. Since we were crucified with Christ, when we are tempted we can simply "play dead" in Him.

4. Praying for the lost when we are tempted takes our mind off ourselves and quickly moves us into the role of intercessors.

---

### Personal Application

1. When people have been accustomed to doing the wrong thing almost by instinct, how do they go about recognizing and resisting temptation?

2. Implement step 8 as suggested or customize it to fit your circumstances. Which model works best for you?

---

### Prayer

Holy Father, it is thrilling when we get the big picture. We can see now what You meant when You said there would not be a temptation that would be so difficult but You had already provided a way for us to resist it successfully.

The problem, Lord, is that we are more accustomed to losing to temptation than we are to resisting it. Resisting temptation is not something that comes naturally to us. We ask that the Holy Spirit alert us so we can recognize when the devil is targeting us and that He be with us as we take the appropriate evasive action.

We are thankful that although the devil works 24 hours a day, seven days a week, to cause us to fall, You have given us the Spirit and as many angels as we may need to help us overcome. We are crucified with Christ and can see how dead people don't respond to temptation, but Lord we can't live by playing dead alone. We must also be raised with Jesus in His resurrection. In the power of our resurrected Lord, help us to experience what it is to be winners! Amen.

# Expect to Grow From Pain and Suffering

Perhaps nothing brings us back to reality more than physical suffering and pain, including the enormous grief of losing someone we love. Though we tend to resent it greatly and avoid it at all costs, often it is suffering that is the ultimate reality check.

Ecclesiastes 7:2-4 tells us: "It is better to go to the house of mourning, than to go to the house of feasting: for that is the end of all men; and the living will lay it to his heart. Sorrow is better than laughter: for by the sadness of the countenance the heart is made better. The heart of the wise is in the house of mourning; but the heart of fools is in the house of mirth." Though we could wish it were otherwise, the Christian life does not exempt us from suffering.

I am thankful that up to now I have enjoyed good health. Except for a cold now and then and maybe a bout with the flu every couple years, I have had few physical problems.

Some time ago, though, I had an incident of what medical science refers to as adhesive capsulitis. Now, I realize that a case of adhesive capsulitis is not the end of the world. It is nothing like the pain that many people struggle with daily from a back problem, or like the crippling pain of rheumatism or arthritis. I feel that I am hardly qualified to discuss the matter of pain except that it was my own experience, and for me it was important to the extent that I had to suffer through it.

My shoulder seemed to be going from bad to worse. Up until that time no doctor had diagnosed my problem. I had only my suspicions. But I finally went to my doctor and he prescribed an MRI. The specialist took one look at the results and confirmed that I had adhesive capsulitis, or frozen shoulder. He gave me a shot to relieve the pain, but its effect soon wore off and things returned to where I had started.

I wanted to know what I was in for, so I went to the Internet and looked up the word "adhesive capsulitis." The computer search found a number of articles and even some illustrations in living color. The articles said that medical science does not know its cause, only that it is painful, especially at night. I could surely vouch for that. I would wake up at night with sheets of pain coursing down my arm. I would have to reach over with my other arm, lift up the affected arm, and rotate it slowly around. For some reason that would make it feel better. The information on the Web page said that the condition could last seven years, and during that time I might lose the ability to move my arm. When I read that, I began to see the problem as something that might for all intents and purposes turn into a permanent disability.

I don't know what you are like spiritually when you get sick. When I am ill I don't particularly feel like praying for myself. It rather takes my spiritual breath away. You would think that being sick would make a person more spiritual. In my case I wouldn't exactly describe it that way. Sickness and pain drain me so much that it even takes an effort to pray.

I think that may be why the book of James says that the sick should call for the elders (James 5:14). I can see how this would be necessary. When we are ill it takes so much out of us that we need others to take up the spiritual slack. After all, Scripture says that we ought to bear each other's burden, and sickness is a big burden (Gal. 6:2).

You will probably consider this strange, but when I am sick it makes me think of all the other ill people in the world. We often don't pay them any attention until we or someone we love gets into that condition.

One summer a friend of mine somehow rolled the lawn mower back over his foot and cut off one of his big toes. He told me that after the accident he discovered to his surprise that many people had had a similar experience. He was just never aware of it before. Although there are always a lot of people who are sick, I don't seem to notice it until I become ill myself, and then I am suddenly aware of just how much pain and suffering really exists in our world.

The point I want to share with you is that when I suffered so much pain with my arm it made me aware of other people just like me who also were living with a lot of pain. They were, in fact, enduring pain before I myself became a card-carrying member of the pain club, and many are still members, even though my membership has run out for the time being.

If you ever think you are the only one who has problems, just share yours and you will be surprised at what you hear. I think this is what it means in the Scripture when it says that we will encounter no trial that isn't also common to everybody else (1 Cor. 10:13). It means that to a great extent life is fairly generic as far as pain and suffering are concerned.

The next time you look at the obituaries, just project down in time and you will find my name there, and one day yours will appear too. As Scripture reminds us, we all will die (Heb. 9:27). Why, I was looking at my birth certificate the other day, and can you believe it has an expiration date! (I am only kidding, of course, but it is really true isn't it?) So I find that when I am sick it doesn't particularly make me spiritually enthusiastic, but it does make me aware of other suffering people and of my own mortality.

Let me tell you what I did while I was going through my shoulder problem. Please don't get the idea that I was enjoying the pain. It was as much pain as I remember ever having been through. But I asked the Lord to use the pain of the frozen shoulder to make me be more compassionate toward the people who suffer all the time. By then I had begun to believe I was going to be that way the rest of my life. *Why should I complain?* I thought to myself. *After all, there are other people who are permanently disabled.*

If God hadn't seen fit to heal them, then who did I think I was that He should heal me? Romans 8:17 says: "And if children, then heirs; heirs of God, and joint-heirs with Christ; if so be that we suffer with him, that we may be also glorified together." I took that to mean that we can expect to suffer. First Peter 4:1 declares: "Forasmuch then as Christ hath suffered for us in the flesh, arm yourselves likewise with the same mind: for he that hath suffered in the flesh hath ceased from sin." This passage told me that suffering can actually bring character development.

So I began to pray, "Lord, my arm is really hurting me. You promised You would not let something be so bad we couldn't bear it. So, Lord, if my arm is going to hurt, then please give me the strength to be able to stand it without getting discouraged."

Then I prayed, "Father, I don't know how long this is going to last, but one thing I want. I long to be compassionate. Forgive me for not noticing the hurting people until now. Please give special grace to the people who are suffering the terrible pain of cancer, and please, Lord, comfort the old people twisted by the pain of arthritis and rheumatism."

In Matthew 6:33 Jesus told us to seek first the kingdom of God and His righteousness. You will discover that when we do that we will have a price to pay, and that price may very well be suffering. It was for Jesus, and it will be for us (1 Peter 5:10).

On the other hand, when we suffer, something wonderful happens—suddenly we begin to know from experience what it means when it says that all things work together for good for those who love God (Rom. 8:28).

If you are expecting to move forward in the Christian life only when things go well, then unless you are completely different from the rest of us you will find yourself stuck in the mud of life's vicissitudes—or even worse, sliding spiritually downhill.

When we commit ourselves to seek God and His righteousness we will know firsthand what it means that nothing will separate us from His love. "What shall we then say to these things? If God be for us, who can be against us? He that spared not his own Son, but delivered him up for us all, how shall he not with him also freely give us all things? Who shall lay any thing to the charge of God's elect? It is God that justifieth. Who is he that condemneth? It is Christ that died, yea rather, that is risen again, who is even at the right hand of God, who also maketh intercession for us. Who shall separate us from the love of Christ? shall tribulation, or distress, or persecution, or famine, or nakedness, or peril, or sword? As it is written, For thy sake we are killed all the day long; we are accounted as sheep for the slaughter.

"Nay, in all these things we are more than conquerors through him that loved us. For I am persuaded, that neither death, nor life, nor angels, nor principalities, nor powers, nor things present, nor things to come, nor height, nor depth, nor any other creature, shall be able to separate us from the love of God, which is in Christ Jesus our Lord" (verses 31-39).

The apostle Peter observes that "it is better, if the will of God be so, that ye suffer for well doing, than for evil doing" (1 Peter 3:17). I believe this text assures us that there is such a thing as needless suffering.

Though I was praying that the Lord would use my frozen shoulder to make me compassionate and to bring me closer to Him, I did ask myself if I might have done something to cause the problem. I have had the problem in both shoulders now. In the first case I almost lost the use of my left arm. It may be just a coincidence, but it seems to me that I have noticed a common element in both incidents.

In both cases I began to feel symptoms shortly after I used some long pruning nippers. The nippers are about three feet long, and I had to work with my arms fully extended. And if I remember right, I was leaning over the edge of our roof trying to cut some branches. I don't know much about physics, but I think this would translate into some serious pressure on my shoulders. As I operated the nippers the problem was likely compounded by the twisting motion as I cut the branches. Since I even so much as suspect that this could be the cause of my problem, I'm sure I'll change my method of cutting branches from the roof.

The episode with my arm was bad. It cost a lot of money. Since the disease has no known cure, you may be assured that I will make sure that I don't knowingly contribute to the problem in the future.

Nevertheless, even when we have been negligent the Lord has promised to be with us in our suffering. He has told us we will suffer while we are here on this earth, but He will not leave us to bear it alone (Heb. 13:5). Even better, He will give us strength to get through it.

It is a human tendency to make God responsible when we or a loved one suffer. Undoubtedly God is sovereign, and all that happens results from His permission. However, He has instituted certain laws that govern our existence and rarely interferes or makes exception when we violate those rules. To do so would put the planet into more chaos than it is already in.

The biblical passages that say the Lord chastens us (Heb.12:7) puzzle many people. Our understanding of the word usually involves punishment. I looked up the word "chastening" in the Greek concordance. The meaning of *paideia* helped me to get the big picture. The word refers to the whole training and education of children. Of course, training and educating our children includes reproof and punishment, but we must see God not so much picking us out for punishment but simply letting the laws of nature take their course. We are born into a continuum of human existence, and it is a natural law that whatever we sow, or our parents sow, or the other members of our family sow, or even the community sows, we will reap the results. It does not rule out the possibility that God will interfere and work a miracle now and then. To use a ridiculous illustration, we must not presumptuously jump off the roof and as we fall pray we will not be hurt.

The people in the time of Jesus believed that if something bad happened to a person it was always a punishment they deserved for something they had done. Jesus set the record straight (Luke 13:1-5; John 9:1-3). He said it was not necessarily so. Caleb and Joshua paid the price of 40 years in the desert for a sin they were not guilty of. Scripture nowhere declares that the child of God will be free of pain and suffering, but it does teach that God is continually training us in good times and bad, and in the end all things will work together for good for those who love God (Rom. 8:28).

The year I struggled with the shoulder problem was hard for me, but it could have been worse. One time a fellow pastor and I visited a church member. As we sat in the living room my friend asked the woman how her son was doing. She replied he was studying for his final exams. I thought nothing of it until we were about to leave and the mother asked us if we wanted to say hello to Johnny. We turned into the first bedroom on the right and saw a young man in his 20s lying on his bed, propped up on his elbows and studying a book. I wondered momentarily why he had not come out to greet us before this. When he extended his hand I could see it was somewhat misshapen. It was then I saw the wheelchair in the corner. Johnny was paralyzed from the waist down as a result of a diving accident. As we visited, the young man said something I have never forgotten: "I feel so sorry for people less fortunate than I am." It reminded me of an old saying: "I complained I had no shoes until I saw a man who had no feet."

I learned much though this experience and expect to learn a lot more before this life is over. Yet I am not discouraged or fearful. Though I don't know what the future holds, the words of our Lord ring in my ears. He said that in this world we will have trouble. But don't give up, because "I have overcome the world" (John 16:33).

---

### What Is Important to Know

1. In this life we must expect to suffer. The mortality rate for the human race is 100 percent. This knowledge should not make us despair but realize that the coming of Jesus is our only hope.

2. Character is built on suffering.

3. One prayer God will always answer yes to is when we ask Him to give us the grace to get through our suffering.

4. If Christians were exempt from suffering, it would attract the greatest number of "rice Christians" the world has ever seen.

---

### Personal Application

1. How have you reacted to the pain and suffering in your life? How has it affected your relationship with Jesus?

2. When we are feeling OK and those we love are OK for the moment, what can we do to keep from forgetting the suffering of others?

---

### Prayer

Our Father in heaven, the experience of pain and suffering is very real. It has touched or will touch all of us in some way. When we or the people we love are healthy and well we often don't notice the suffering around us or we soon forget. As we see a person whose fingers are twisted with arthritis we often don't feel the ongoing pain they endure or realize how they have struggled with it.

Lord, please lead us into a spirit of compassion.

Another thing, Father. We thought that if we did everything right we wouldn't have to suffer. Help us to know that suffering is the nature of the present life and give us, as You have promised, Your grace to be able to bear it. When we feel our own pain or the pain of others it makes us really long for Your coming. Maranatha!

# Expect to Develop a Healthy Lifestyle–1

I had come to New York City on business and was in a taxi on my way to a meeting. A taxi driver makes money from fares and then has to pay licensing fees and the maintenance of the vehicle from them. As we rode along through the traffic I wondered how long a cab would last before its owner would need to buy a new one.

"How many miles do you put on your taxi?" I asked my driver.

Without hesitation he replied, "Two hundred and fifty thousand."

*Isn't that incredible?* I thought. *If I could get a quarter of a million miles on my car that would be great.* "How do you do it? How do you get it to last so long?"

"I change the oil," he replied.

When I heard this it surprised me. It was so simple. I had assumed that he would tell me about some new mechanical breakthrough. I already knew about changing the oil.

Of course we know. But although a vehicle is probably the second most expensive investment we will ever make (after a house), too often we do not change the oil regularly until the day comes when we have trouble with the car, and then we blame everything and everybody but ourselves. The truth, though, is that we weren't maintaining the car as the manual told us to.

I suspect we often do this with our bodies as well, especially when we are young. Young people think they will always stay young. Though for a time it may seem we are immortal and will live forever, the fact is that we won't. Most people don't give their health a thought until something goes wrong.

Have you ever noticed who generally gets the blame when we get sick? God. If that is not the case, then why do we pray, "Lord, why did You let this happen to me?" And of course if God would talk to us, He would tell us He didn't do it.

We would feel a little embarrassed and would conclude then that it must have been the devil. But the devil with a fiendish grin would say, "I would like to have done it, but I didn't do it either. You did it to yourself." Researchers have estimated that 80 percent of the things killing us result from our own lifestyles.

On another occasion I was in New York City visiting the health-screening program the Greater New York Conference sponsors. On that early-April day we visited the borough of Queens.

A young woman entered the van to have her blood pressure checked, and we began to talk together about health. She said she used to weigh 230 pounds. I didn't ask her how much she had lost, but I guessed it might have been about 100 pounds. "How did you lose that weight?" I inquired.

"Through prayer," she replied.

Now, that was a new one. I had heard of all kinds of weight-loss programs, but never getting rid of weight through prayer. Thinking that I had heard wrong, I asked her again. Once more she said she had done it through prayer. I was too embarrassed to ask for details, so I said no more about it.

One day shortly afterward I received a letter from my dad, a retired minister. When he sends me letters they sometimes have great sermon ideas in them. Occasionally they even contain little sermonettes. In that particular letter my father was writing about the Holy Spirit.

He explained that generally when we talk about the Holy Spirit we refer particularly to the gifts of the Spirit, a distinction I hadn't thought of before. If being able to do miracles means that you automatically have the gifts of the Spirit, he continued, then Judas must have had the gifts, and for that matter the devil, too, because even he is able to do miracles (Rev. 16:14).

The point he was making was that the gifts of the Spirit can be counterfeited. So he suggested it would be better if we focused more on the fruit of the Spirit before we do the gifts of the Spirit. What Dad said me made me think. He went on to point out that God's gift to us of the fruit of the Spirit is what gets us ready to go to heaven. I believe he is right.

After I read the letter I got my Bible and turned to Galatians 5, the chapter that talks about the fruit of the Spirit. There in verses 22 and 23 was the list. "But the fruit of the Spirit is love, joy, peace, longsuffering, gentleness, goodness, faith, meekness, temperance."

That last fruit (temperance) really jumped out at me. Another word for it is self-control. I had prayed for love and all the rest, but I guess that because self-control is at the end of the list I had never gotten down that far. I couldn't remember a time when I had prayed for self-control. After doing a quick inventory of my own life, I concluded that in many ways my life was out of control. The most obvious indication was the way I eat.

You see, I am a type A personality. I don't know if we type A's are all the same, but one of my characteristics is that I tend to eat too much and too fast. I will consume two plates of food while you are eating one. A person who eats fast doesn't chew their food very well—they don't have time.

In addition, we choke ourselves to death if we don't drink like a fish. And so when we have had two or three plates of food and have drunk a quart of liquid, we walk away from the table feeling guilty. Have you ever gotten up from the table feeling that way?

So as I did an inventory on myself I could see that I was eating too much and too fast. Now, I could make a lot of excuses, such as that the problem is my stomach. Unfortunately, I got my stomach when I was born, and it is the only one I will ever have. I do not have much hope of obtaining a new stomach. Or I could claim that I overeat because my wife is the best cook in the world, and if you had to eat her food you would pig out too. All of us make similar excuses for being what we are.

Finally I had to admit that in my case, at least, it was not my stomach or my wife's cooking that was the problem, but my lack of self-control. I could not blame the supermarket or the refrigerator or the stove—only myself.

Then it occurred to me what the young woman on the van had been talking about when she said she had lost weight through prayer. I could see that although Jesus will not give us a new stomach or a new wife, He has promised to give us a new heart. That is what the promise of the fruit of the Spirit is all about. So I began to pray that God would give me self-control.

I was the kind of person who, when I came home from work at night, would take off my suit and throw it on the bed. Then I would put on my work clothes or other casual clothes for the evening. I don't remember my wife ever mentioning to me that I ought to hang up my clothes. She just went along through the years hanging them up for me.

One day when I came home from work it suddenly occurred to me, *Why not hang up your suit?* So I went to the closet, found a hanger, hung up my clothes, and continued to do so for several days.

My wife and I share a closet. Her clothes are on one side and mine are on the other. One day when I went to the closet to hang up my suit I noticed something. My wife's clothes hung in a neat row, and her shoes were all in a row facing the same direction. But my side of the closet was something else. The clothes were crooked from being jostled around when I would take my shirts or suits down. My shoes pointed every which way.

So I hung all my slacks together in a row. Next I placed the shirts in a row. Then I hung the jackets together, each facing the same way. I was praying for self-control, and now my life was beginning to slow down so I could actually catch up with myself.

One day I went out to the garage and noticed that it was a mess. We had lived in the house for only three years, but stuff lay everywhere. I could never find my hammer or other tools. Did you ever have that problem? That's because we people who are out of control never put things back where they belong. And so I looked at the garage that day and declared that something had to be done.

An old rickety tool bench had come with the house. Deciding to fix it up, I bought some plywood, used it to nail the bench back together, and painted everything. Then I moved it over to one corner of the garage.

Buying a pegboard and little hooks to go with it, I began to hang up the hammers and wrenches and screwdrivers. Instantly I discovered I had more hammers than I needed. You see, when you just throw hammers around, you lose them. And then when you need one, you have to go out and buy another. Suddenly out there in the garage I began to see there could be a place for everything, and so I put everything in its place. What was going on? I wasn't reading a book on how to hang up clothes or how to keep the garage clean. My wife wasn't nagging me either. I was praying God would give me self-control, and the result was changing my lifestyle.

Let me tell you what else happened to me. I lost about 20 pounds. Have you figured out yet what was happening? Our fight must not be against calories or cookies but rather our tendency to be out of control. Now I knew what the woman on the van was trying to tell me. I also appreciated the letter I received from my dad. My battle is not over. Once a type A, always a type A—at least as far as I am concerned. But there is hope for us. As sons and daughters of

God we have a promise that if we ask, He will give us just what we need (Luke 11:9).

## What Is Important to Know

1. We should not blame God when we neglect to follow the principles of health and then become ill.

2. It is possible that a person could manifest gifts of the Spirit and still not be on God's side. The gifts of the Spirit can be counterfeited.

3. When we see our problems as originating inside us we are finally in a condition to receive help, because God is in the business of giving us a new heart.

## Personal Application

1. What are several reasons our health is important?

2. In what specific ways might your life change if you began to pray for the Lord to give you self-control?

## Prayer

Dear Lord, You know how sometimes some of us live so fast it is hard for us to slow down enough to let the Holy Spirit do His work in our lives. We are thankful that You have promised to give us the fruit of the Spirit if we will ask. Also we see now how important prayer is if we are going to begin to experience the blessings that Jesus purchased for us on the cross.

Forgive us for getting carried away with so many things and in so many ways. Please continue to give to those of us whose personalities are so susceptible to busyness the gift of self-control. We know that losing a little weight or hanging up our clothes is nice, but the best part of all is the knowledge that You are working much deeper in our hearts and helping us reflect Jesus, who loves us so much and in whose name we pray. Amen.

# Expect to Develop a Healthy Lifestyle–2

God has taught us how to be happy and healthy. But—I must say this very carefully and I don't know exactly how it happened—in some places a spirit of fanaticism has taken over the health message.

A person came up to me one time and asked, "Do you want to be a member of the 144,000?"

What can you say to a question like that? You have to say yes, but you know there must be more to come. So I said I did. Then the individual held up a copy of the book *Counsels on Diets and Foods* and said, "Well, then, here is the translation diet."

How would that make you feel? This kind of approach doesn't make you want to get into health or be a member of the 144,000. We don't know the whole story yet, but this much we know—God will not translate the 144,000 because of their diet. They will be translated because they surrendered their hearts and lives to the Lord Jesus Christ. A person can be a vegan and worship Buddha.

For this reason I tell people, Don't give up eggs—reduce their consumption; but definitely give up fornication. Do you see the difference? Now, if you are concerned about cholesterol, you'd better consider the matter of eggs. Eggs are loaded with cholesterol. Anyone who is serious about keeping their veins unclogged will not want to have four eggs for breakfast every day. So we should go easy on eggs. You may never eat another egg as long as you live—that's up to you. But if along the way you should happen to eat an egg sandwich sometime, you won't have to be rebaptized. Isn't that good news?

For the same reason, I say don't give up cheese—just cut back on it. But we must give up lying. If you are serious about fat in your diet, you are going to have to consider the matter of cheese and deal with it accordingly. Medical research suggests that fat is one of the principal causes of diabetes, and cheese has a high fat content. Now, if you start to deal with cheese, again you may never eat another bite of it for the rest of your life. However, if you happen to see someone else eating a cheese sandwich, you won't criticize them (see Ps. 15:3).

God has given us wonderful and necessary information as to how we can live in harmony with the laws of health. He desires that within the context of our mortality and the ravages of sin upon our bodies we be in optimum health. "Beloved, I wish above all things that thou mayest prosper and be in health" (3 John 2). However, in the pursuit of good health what we need to address first is the matter of self-control. I can put you on a guilt trip and you can put me on a guilt trip, and afterward we can go and pig out anyway. The first thing we need before we even have a class in nutrition is a new heart. The Lord graciously leads us in every aspect of our lives. It is when we try to get ahead of Him or fail to put first things first that we easily can get out of balance, lose perspective, and miss the big picture.

But here we face a danger. After I had started taking the principles of health seriously I began to see an even worse problem manifesting itself in my life, and that was to look at other people who were eating the things I had given up as "lesser life forms." Though I had "gotten the victory" over cookies, I now was guilty of the greatest sin of all—the one that Jesus condemned every time He saw it—the sin of spiritual pride.

When I realized the point I had come to, I could see that my problem had never been the cookies. The difficulty was that I couldn't eat just two. So I had gone from the extreme of eating the whole box to "getting victory over cookies." It dawned on me one day that it was easier to give up cookies entirely than to eat just two or three.

Someone may ask, "But what about the sugar and fat?" Please think along with me now. Stealing is wrong wherever you find it. If sugar were morally wrong like stealing, it would be wrong in orange juice. In the same manner lying is always wrong. But if fat were inherently evil it would be wrong wherever you find it, including in an avocado. Another thing, when we process foods we tend to unbalance their nutritive value and in the process cause the price to go up. The difference in the nutritional value of a baked potato and a bag of potato chips is obvious, as is the matter of their respective prices. In principle, the closer we come to eating things as God gave them, the better, not only for nutrition and health but for our pocketbook as well.

We often look at health only in terms of what we eat or don't eat. If an angel were to come down from heaven and put all of the elements that comprise a healthy lifestyle on a table and then instruct us that we could take only one, do you know which one we should choose? Exercise. To paraphrase a text, exercise covers a multitude of other sins against the laws of health. Our forebears may have had diets that were high in fat and cholesterol, but they worked it off walking behind a horse-drawn plow or washing the family clothes on a scrub board.

Another element we need in our lives is water. When the car runs out of water, the engine burns up. We make our bodies ineffective and to some extent poison ourselves by not drinking enough water. By the way, when you really get thirsty your body is not calling for a bottle of pop. You can take your water in the form of pop if you want to, but what your body needs is water. If we make a habit of obtaining our water in the form of soft drinks, we will surely add other problems.

It's not easy to eat simple foods, because we have jaded appetites. That is why we need to pray for self-control. You may think you have gone too far and can't turn back, but it is never too late to get a new start. Do you know how long it takes to establish a new habit in your life? Approximately 30 days. You can decide now that you want some changes in your life, and if you'll be patient, the Lord will help you to establish new habits after only about a month.

Someone has said that good health is not everything, but without it everything is nothing. God made us to be healthy. But we must remember that the foundation upon which the principles of health must rest is self-control.

My favorite text on the subject of health is one you can use too. "Whether therefore ye eat, or drink, or whatsoever ye do, do all to the glory of God" (1 Cor. 10:31). I want my life to be to the glory of God, don't you? I can't provide you self-control, nor can you give it to me. If we don't have it, then, where are we going to get it? From God, who is waiting to offer it to us if we will but ask Him for it.

In addition, we must not assume that self-control is something that God will present to us just once and that we will never need to ask Him for it again. I know from experience that I must pray for self-control often. (By the way, if anybody ever tells you they have arrived spiritually, don't believe them. The only people who have arrived are the dead!) Every now and then when I sit down to eat I have to pray, "Lord, help me to eat slowly," or "Lord, help me to chew my food." Sometimes I have to pray that He will give me the self-control I need to go out and get some exercise.

But there is nothing more fun than seeing the Lord work in your life, and nothing less enjoyable than knowing your life is out of control. Without doubt the health message that God has so graciously given us can make sense and be kept in perspective only as we ask for and receive the wonderful gift of self-control. "I am come that they might have life," Jesus said, "and that they might have it more abundantly" (John 10:10).

## What Is Important to Know

1. Preparing for the coming of Jesus is not just about diet. Millions of people who worship idols are vegetarians, and millions who don't drink alcohol reject Jesus as the Son of God.

2. In the area of health it is easy to go from one extreme to the next. Spiritual pride and hypocrisy can easily infect those who advocate the health message (and they even sneak a cookie now and then).

3. A person who appreciates what Jesus has done and is doing in their lives will be sensitive to healthful living as an opportunity to glorify God.

4. Those who feel that they have it all together as far as healthful living is concerned should still pray for self-control. It may affect the way they treat their spouse and children.

## Personal Application

1. As you pray for self-control, what other areas of your life do you see being affected in addition to health?

2. If we have been to one extreme in the past in the area of healthful living, what can we do now to keep from going to the other extreme?

## Prayer

Wonderful Father, thank You for the priceless gift that You have given us in Jesus Christ our Lord. As we see our need and as we look at Him we understand that He is the only way we can have the abundant life He has promised us.

Lord, we recognize that because we get out of control we can distort even the good things that You have given us. We can focus on one piece of the puzzle and forget what the whole picture is supposed to look like. Please continue to give us the self-control we need not only to meet the challenge of living a healthy lifestyle but also the self-control we need for every other activity of our lives. We can see You working in our lives. But we also recognize that You are not finished with us yet. We pray that You who have begun Your good work in us will complete it in every way through the love and grace of Jesus Christ, in whose name we pray. Amen.

# Expect the Sabbath to Be Special—1

For some the Sabbath has definitely not met their expectations. It is frustrating at best and boring at worst. For many the day is not the blessing it was said to be but rather a guilt trip. If you were to ask the average person how they keep the Sabbath, they would tell you 20 things they shouldn't do. A friend confessed that one time his neighbor asked him how he observed the Sabbath. "Well," he relied, "we don't read the newspaper . . ."

To make matters even more complicated, today many wives work outside the home and husbands may commute 75 miles a day. In some cases we might not even get home from work until after sundown. It comes as no surprise, then, that in general we don't get ready for the Sabbath the way we used to. When I was a child we polished our shoes and pressed our clothes on Friday. I can remember mother cleaning the house and baking and cooking, and when the sun was about to set she called us together and we sat down for worship.

A person who hadn't been an Adventist for very long said to me, "When I became an Adventist, nobody ever told me what to do on Sabbath, so I have just been sort of winging it." Unfortunately some of us have been Adventists all our lives but still are winging it.

For many people the Sabbath amounts to little more than an interruption in their lives. Have you ever been driving down the highway in a hurry to get to an appointment? Fortunately the lights seem to be all green in your favor. That is good, because you realize you have only five minutes to get where you are going. But as you approach an intersection the light turns red just as you get there. You feel irritated, and fear you are going to be late for your appointment. Glancing at your watch, you wonder if the light is ever going to change. After what seems to be an eternity the light changes, but the car in front of you doesn't move. You lay on the horn.

For many of us the Sabbath is like a red light in our lives. Friday comes, and when the sun starts to set we have to put on the brakes in our life, and even then we often skid into the Sabbath. During Sabbath we often watch the clock, and when sundown comes the tires squeal and we roar back off into life again.

Too many young people consider the Sabbath rather like being in jail. Unable to do anything, they can't wait until sunset. Perhaps when church service lets out some people, instead of attending the church potluck, go to the Olive Garden. A person might ask, "What's wrong with that? I don't get a Sabbath blessing cooking dinner. I would rather let somebody else cook." Others say they get a Sabbath blessing by spending time in the swimming pool, visiting the beach, or sitting around watching a little TV.

I am convicted that Sabbath has something special in it for us, and I want to discover what it is. Hebrews 4:9-11 says that there remains a rest for God's people and calls us to participate in it. Although I don't comprehend all that the text tells us, I am intrigued by the concept. I want to know what it is about. If God has something special for me on Sabbath, I know that I need it.

What is the Sabbath? What's it all about? It has been around for a long time (Gen. 2:2, 3). Some evangelists have called the Sabbath Adam's mother's birthday. Thinking of the Sabbath as a birthday is a nice thought—the birthday of our planet, the birthday of God's creation. But I don't feel totally comfortable with regarding Sabbath as just a birthday. I like to view it as more like a wedding anniversary. Let me explain why.

A birthday involves only one person. On my birthday, who is the center of attention? I am. When they sing "Happy Birthday," it's to me. Let's face it, my birthday celebrates me. So whom do I think of on my birthday? Myself, of course.

On the other hand, a wedding anniversary is something else. An anniversary is not about me—it's about us. This is why I can understand the Sabbath better when I see it as an anniversary. The Sabbath is not about Saturday, but about God and me, God and you. A wedding anniversary is for married people. This is why the Sabbath is not for just anybody. The seventh day, according to Scripture, is a sign between God and those who serve Him (Ex. 31:13). If people don't serve God or have Jesus as the Lord of their lives, then the Sabbath is not for them. When we think about it in this way we understand that the world doesn't need the Sabbath. Sometimes we assume that if we just preach the Sabbath to all the world, we will finish God's mission on earth. No, the Sabbath is not what the world needs first—it needs Jesus first. The Sabbath blessing comes after a person makes a commitment to Jesus, just as the wedding anniversary follows after you get married. It becomes our anniversary. Scripture teaches that the Sabbath symbolizes that Jesus is the Lord of our lives (Luke 6:5).

When you really love someone, an anniversary can be a special and exciting event. But the problem with wedding anniversaries is that they occur only once a year. Fortunately, God knew we needed more than once-a-year quality time with Him. For that reason He has given us an anniversary every seven days. We keep our noses to the grindstone six days, but on the seventh day we are free to rest (Ex. 20:8-11).

I don't know why it is so easy to get into the mind-set that God takes away something good from us when the Sabbath arrives each week. At least some look at it that way. We don't regard our anniversary that way, however. If it's your anniversary and you and your wife are planning to go out, and I should come along and say, "Hey, why don't you come on over to my place tonight?" you would immediately reply, "No, thank you."

"What's the matter; don't you like me?" I might protest.

You would respond, "I like you, all right, but tonight is for my wife/husband, and we are going out. It's our anniversary." Can you see it then? The Sabbath is our time with God. It belongs to us. And it is more than a day off.

No, the Sabbath isn't God taking something away from us. It's the world that wants to steal the Sabbath. We must not let it happen. Have you been working hard this week? I want to tell you some good news: you are only six days or less away from being set free from the grind. We can survive if we know we don't have to take it for more than six days. A person can work hard for six days. But working hard for seven days invalidates our warranty. Jesus invites all of us who are weary to find rest in Him (Matt. 11:28). I need that rest—I really do. For this reason I am so thankful that a rest still remains for God's people.

The question that now comes to mind involves how we are going to get the most benefit from this day that God has given us. I am going to share with you what I believe is a good guideline. Remember, the Sabbath is not about the clock or the calendar, but about our relationship to God. The day we celebrate our anniversary is significant because it concerns my wife and me. So if the Sabbath is going to be meaningful, it must be rise from our commitment to Jesus.

Suppose that our anniversary (which happens to be on June 19) is approaching and my wife asks, "Honey, what are we going to do for our anniversary?" And further, she suggests, "Why don't we go out to eat?"

I might say, "Let's do that."

Then she adds, "You know, we have been working so hard lately it will be nice to be alone for a change, just the two of us."

"What do you mean, alone?" I protest. "I was going to bring someone."

"Who were you going to bring?"

"Alice. She's in town this week."

"Who?" my wife asks incredulously. "That's your old girl-friend from academy days! You're going to bring *her* on our wedding anniversary?"

Ridiculous, isn't it? But can you see the principle involved? God asks us not to love the world or the things associated with it (1 John 2:15), and elsewhere Scripture tells that friendship with the world is hostility toward God (James 4:4). That means when God gave us the Sabbath He asked for quality time. The time is just for Him and us. So when you consider what is appropriate to do on this special day, a good principle to follow is Don't bring along your old boyfriends and girlfriends. This is why I don't go to the beach on Sabbath. The beach is for other days, other times, but not our Sabbath anniversary. And I don't go out to eat on the Sabbath, because the environment is not just us. It seems to me that as much as possible we should be in the company of those who are also celebrating the anniversary as we are.

If I were to insist on bringing my old girlfriends to my wedding anniversary, my wife would begin to wonder whether I really care about her. In a similar manner, if we spend Sabbath associating with the world and treat it only as a day off, it raises the question of whether we really value our relationship with God.

I believe this is what Isaiah 58:13, 14 has in mind. "If thou turn away thy foot from the Sabbath, from doing thy pleasure on my holy day; and call the Sabbath a delight, the holy of the Lord, honourable; and shalt honour Him, not doing thine own ways, nor finding thine own pleasure, nor speaking thine own words: then shalt thou delight thyself in the Lord." That is pretty clear, isn't it?

### What Is Important to Know

1. The Sabbath doesn't take anything from us—rather, it gives.

2. The Sabbath is about a relationship we have with Jesus. If the relationship is missing, the Sabbath will have little significance except maybe as a day off.

3. Although I am married every day, my anniversary is only one day a year. Although we are committed to Jesus as our Creator and Saviour every day, only one day is the sign of this relationship—the seventh day of the week.

### Personal Application

1. Could there be a correlation between the fact that we are spending less time with the people in our lives that really matter, i.e., our families, and the reality that we are also spending less quality time with God? What would be the connection?

2. How will keeping the spirit of the Sabbath affect the specific ways we observe it? (Does the spirit of the law do away with the letter of the law?)

### Prayer

Dear Father in heaven, please forgive us for getting so wrapped up in the things of our world that we sometimes resent having to stop and give You quality time. Lord, You have told us in Your Word that even in modern life You provide a rest for Your people. Probably a lot of our stress comes from the fact that we are not entering into that rest the way You meant for us to.

Forgive us for taking along old "girlfriends/boyfriends" when You meant for it to be just us. You told us in the fourth commandment to remember the Sabbath. That is important, Lord, because we tend to forget so easily. Convict us more and more of this special time, we ask in Jesus' name. Amen.

# Expect the Sabbath to Be Special–2

We usually have a good idea of what we should not do on Sabbath. As the man told his neighbor, we don't read the newspaper. Now that we have spent all these years learning what not to do, the challenge we face is how we can honor God on the Sabbath. Some years ago I began to consider this question seriously. Since God has a special rest for those who choose the Sabbath, I felt I was missing something and determined to do what I could through the power of the Holy Spirit to enter into that rest in practical ways.

I am convinced that the success we have in honoring the Sabbath hours will depend on our planning in advance what we will do during the day of rest. We decide beforehand what we are going to do on our vacation that we generally take only once a year. Also we prepare for other events important to us. The Sabbath is difficult for many for the simple reason they do not make plans for it. As a result they have come to see it not as a destination but as a red light. It is important to have a plan and follow it.

Whole books have described how to observe the Sabbath so that its 24 hours will be to the glory of the Lord of the Sabbath. I want to share some of the things we personally have discovered that make the Sabbath meaningful. Once we see the Sabbath as something between God and us, and once we begin to plan beforehand how we will keep it, we will discover that the possibilities for honoring Jesus on His day are endless.

Did you know it is possible to receive a double blessing from the Sabbath? One comes from the actual Sabbath hours and the other from getting ready for the Sabbath to arrive. My wife and I have four children and seven grandchildren. Two of the families live in another state, so you can imagine we are happy when they are able to visit us. My wife spends several days before their expected arrival getting the rooms where they will stay ready and doing whatever special grocery shopping is necessary. We have discovered that the fun we have when our children visit us begins even before they arrive.

In our home getting ready for the Sabbath begins in earnest on Thursday. My wife does her grocery shopping after work that day and also some of the deep cleaning of the house. Since my office closes early on Fridays it allows me to be responsible for getting the last-minute things done before Sabbath. I run the vacuum cleaner and finish whatever cleaning remains from Thursday night. Friday afternoon is wind-down time. I prefer not to start new projects during that time but to steer things toward the coming of sunset.

We know the approximate times our children and grandchildren from out of town will arrive, and if it is by air, we make sure we are there to meet them when they come down the sky-bridge at the airport. A similar principle applies to the Sabbath. If it is not your custom yet to be there on your knees talking to Jesus as the Sabbath hours begin, I urge you to try it. It is something we look forward to all week long.

On Friday nights our family has followed the custom for more than 12 years of having our Friday supper in the dining room. After spreading a nice tablecloth on the table, we set the table with our best dishes and table service. I help make it as attractive as I can, napkins and all. Then I put hymnals at each place. I do it whether we are alone or have visitors. Before we eat we sit around the table and sing. When it is just my wife and me we sound OK, but when any of our children are there or if we happen to have company to give it a little harmony, it sounds very nice. First we sing for perhaps five minutes; then we do a responsive reading. After that we sing "Don't Forget the Sabbath."

On the table we have seven-day wax prayer candles that we buy at the supermarket and place in a tall glass so they don't drip. I like having candles in the house on Friday night. After all, Jesus is the Light of the world, and He tells us to let our light shine. I also have candles in the family room, and I light them about two hours before the sun goes down. It's fun to have traditions. They make an occasion really special.

After we sing "Don't Forget the Sabbath," we repeat together the Sabbath commandment, then we pray and eat. Guess what special food we eat every Friday night? Pizza! My wife makes it with a prepared crust or maybe on a round of pita bread. When we lived overseas she used to make it from scratch from the sauce up. But now she gets things here and there and puts it together—nothing fancy or difficult or expensive. When our children come home to visit, they want to have mama's pizza on Friday night. By the way, you can make a vegan pizza if you want. So that's the way Friday evening goes for us.

Honoring God on Sabbath morning is not too difficult, inasmuch as the morning hours are occupied by Sabbath school and church. Unfortunately some neglect to attend church in spite of the fact that Scripture tells us we ought to be there (Heb. 10:25). I have heard some say they get a bigger blessing walking in the woods or along the beach than they do going to church. I am sure that being alone with God in nature does bring a blessing and inspiration, but we should not see it as a substitute for meeting with the body of Christ (Matt. 18:20).

Many church members increasingly stay away from Sabbath school. There may be two reasons for this. First, people like to sleep in on Sabbath morning, and second, sometimes the Sabbath school program has so little planning and preparation that it does not hold anyone's interest. This can become a vicious cycle. As the program quality diminishes, fewer people attend, and with a smaller audience any incentive to improve the program becomes less and less.

On the other hand, in some cultures believers dedicate nearly the whole day to church. Many arrive in the morning and do not return home until Sabbath evening. For them the day is full of worship, fellowship, and missionary activities.

Please don't miss the church experience. If we get sick physically, we call the ambulance to take us to the hospital. But when we get sick spiritually, instead of going to church we usually stay away. When you start feeling as though you want to stay away from church, that's the time to make sure you get there.

Church pretty well takes care of Sabbath morning. But what about Sabbath afternoon? Remember the principle of the anniversary and don't hunt up your old boyfriend or girlfriend ("Love not the world, neither the things that are in the world" [1 John 2:15]). Always keep in mind that you are not the only one honoring God on His day, so it can be an even greater blessing to do things together with other Sabbathkeepers.

Planning is the key to what to do on Sabbath afternoon. If I asked you what you will do Wednesday, you could probably tell me. You might say you are going to get up at such and such a time, have breakfast, go to work, and do such and such. Or if I inquired what you plan for Monday afternoon, you probably could recite your schedule. On the other hand, if someone asks us what we intend for Sabbath afternoon, we often can't think of a thing. "Sleep, I guess," many might answer.

We need to plan our Sabbaths. You might ask what I think about sleeping. A nap would be OK, but we must resist the temptation to sleep all afternoon. Not only do we need physical rest; we need a change of pace. Life can get to be a boring routine. Sabbath can break that routine and give us a new outlook. But if we stay in bed all day Sabbath, Friday will blend into Sunday, and we will have missed the change we so badly need.

The point is we need to think beforehand what we are going to do, and of course it must be in harmony with the guidelines God has given us in His Word (Isa. 58:13, 14).

Oh yes, we should also be careful about Saturday night. We can end up losing a wonderful Sabbath blessing by what we do then. Just like sitting at an intersection waiting for the light to change, we can go speeding down the road at the crack of sundown. Let's leave Sabbath slowly. If Sabbath is the joy and blessing God means for it to be, we are not going to want to let it go the minute the sun goes down. We will want it to depart reluctantly, and when it's gone, we will find ourselves saying, "Oh, I can't wait until it comes back again."

The Sabbath blessing doesn't end with sunset. There remains a rest to the people of God. Jesus' invitation is "Come unto me, all ye that labour and are heavy laden, and I will give you rest" (Matt. 11:28). I need that rest. As we experience growth with the Lord Jesus Christ we can expect that the Sabbath will become more and more significant in our lives. A wedding anniversary doesn't mean much to a couple who have drifted apart. Yet it will become more and more significant to the couple whose love is ever growing and whose appreciation for each other constantly increases.

Let me ask you a personal question. How do you feel about the Sabbath? Do you suspect, as I do, that we have been missing something good? Do you share the feeling in your heart that if there's something special God has for us on that day, you too want to discover it? If that is not the case, it could be that our commitment to Jesus as the Lord of our life has somehow cooled off or we have let life's cares entrap us. When Jesus is Lord of our lives the Sabbath becomes something we are not going to let the world take away.

"There remaineth therefore a rest to the people of God. For he that is entered into his rest, he also hath ceased from his own works, as God did from his. Let us labour therefore to enter into that rest, lest any man fall after the same example of unbelief" (Heb. 4:9-11).

I'm glad the Sabbath doesn't come just once a year. Each week we have another opportunity for a blessing. If you weren't ready for the Sabbath this week when it arrived, you have another chance. And if you didn't plan what you were going to do last Sabbath, begin now to prepare for this Sabbath. One of these days we will enter into that eternal rest in the earth made new. Until then, I invite you here and now to share His Sabbath rest.

## What Is Important to Know

1. Most of us plan how we will use time that we consider important to us. As the Sabbath becomes more significant as a sign of our commitment to Jesus we will become more careful as to how we spend the time with Him.

2. We can enhance the blessing of the Sabbath by being ready for it when it arrives. Also we will find joy in getting ready for it.

3. The hours of the Sabbath are an opportunity to develop family traditions.

4. As Jesus becomes more real to us we will see the Sabbath more and more as a destination and not as a red light.

## Personal Application

1. What would you need to do differently in your way of approaching the Sabbath to be able to see it as a destination and not as a red light?

2. I invited you to be intentional in what you do on Sabbath afternoons. Why not begin this Sabbath!

## Prayer

Father, You who created us and all that is essential for our blessing and enjoyment, we sense that the greatest blessing of all is when we are with You. Though trying to survive occupies our lives here, we are thankful we can escape it each week and rest, and that unlike a vacation that comes only once a year, Sabbath is never more than six days away.

We have a problem, Lord, in that for some of us it is easier to plan our vacation than to arrange the time we will spend with You. We are ashamed that we are often not there when Your special time arrives or that we find ourselves eagerly waiting for Sabbath to end so that we can get back on the road of life.

It is our assurance that You will remedy this as we value more and more our commitment to You. May the Holy Spirit convict us ever more deeply. Help us break loose from the cares of this life so that truly we might experience with joy every Sabbath what it means to enter into Your rest, because You are our God and we are Your people. Amen.

# Expect to Be Different From the Rest

For a number of years during my ministry we lived outside the country of our birth, and then for seven more years my work required me to travel extensively through other countries and cultures. Americans sometimes see their nation as the center of the universe. A story tells of a cruise ship from the United States that had arrived at a port in another country. As the passengers waited to disembark, the ship's officers distributed immigration cards. One passenger returned hers not filled out. When someone asked why, she replied, "Well, the card said it was for foreigners, and I am not a foreigner!"

As I traveled and lived abroad it was an eye-opener to see the people, their countries, and their cultures. To be exposed to their languages was both fascinating and frustrating.

When we first arrived in South America we immediately knew we were in a different country with a different culture, and most difficult of all, a different language. I can remember how helpless I felt and how I used to pray that inasmuch as God was the one who had broken up the universal language at the tower of Babel, would He now please see fit to help me learn the new language. He answered my prayer, and I can now speak Spanish.

What does this have to do with what to expect in the Christian life? The answer is: Everything. In getting the big picture we must understand that in the Christian life we can expect to be different. I could approach this concept from two angles. One could be that when God made us as individuals He threw away the mold. We are one of a kind and therefore make a mistake when we feel that somehow we must be like someone else. Much of our feeling of rejection results from believing that somehow we are not like everybody else. People who feel they are failures are often simply the victim of mass advertising that tells them that unless they eat certain things, drive in certain cars, and dress a certain way they are nobodies.

Scripture advises us that we should not compare ourselves with one another. "For we dare not make ourselves of the number, or compare ourselves with some that commend themselves: but they measuring themselves by themselves, and comparing themselves among themselves, are not wise" (2 Cor. 10:12).

You may never have thought of it this way before, but much of modern advertising is a not-so-subtle put-down of who we are as people and a blatant attempt to put us all in the same mold and make us all look and act the same.

In the first chapter we established that God's purpose for all of us is the same—that we become like Jesus. But that will not make us all identical. When we have the character of Jesus as the foundation of our being we each become truly unique and a marvelous and wonderful manifestation of His creation.

The other aspect to our being different is the one I will attempt to develop in this chapter. It does not focus on the individual uniqueness I have just referred to, but on our collective uniqueness as a group of people who have accepted salvation and in whom God is working.

This emphasis contrasts us with culture. Our culture is the way we live, dress, speak, and work. To a large extent culture is our lifestyle. It is not necessary to remind you that Christian lifestyle is a much-debated topic, and getting into the subject tends to make us disagree and can even disrupt our unity in the body of Christ.

Before we discuss the particulars we need to arrive at the principle that underlies any particular issue. It is a waste of time to discuss a specific matter if we have different definitions of terms and are in reality comparing apples with oranges.

For me, living abroad and seeing other cultures—and even cultures within cultures—helped me understand the hows and whys of the Christian culture.

Southern Asia is one of the richest areas of the world in which to see a potpourri of cultures. We lived some years in the Punjab. Before the partition of India the Punjab was the home of the Sikhs. Sikh men wear a turban. Their hair is long, but they keep it tucked up inside the turban. The men grow a beard, wear silver bangles on their wrist, and carry somewhere on their person a symbolic sword. I also discovered that their last name was most often Singh, a word that means lion.

Then there were the snake charmers. You could recognize them by their dress. Their robe was yellow, as was their turban. Of course, they carried baskets that contained the snakes. When you see a man who looks like that, you don't have to ask him what he does for a living.

Around the world various people groups wear particular costumes. They speak a specific language and have a unique kind of jewelry. All of this gives them identity. A person's culture is often not so much a matter of right or wrong but rather of identity. Remove the identifying marks of the culture, and individuals lose much of their place in their people group.

The implications for the Christian are obvious. Those whom the Lord will sanctify He must first separate (Ex. 20:2) from the world as a whole. In order for God to develop His unique nation it was necessary to take them out of the culture of Egypt and teach them another culture. The history of Israel in the Old Testament is basically a story of what happens when a unique people try to integrate themselves into the dominant culture around them.

In order to maintain its identity a culture or a people group may have customs that are not moral issues but simply ways of life that distinguish them from other groups. I am convinced that this is a valid principle, but it raises a question. Is it reasonable to expect that the sons and daughters of God will look different and live a different lifestyle than those who have not yet accepted salvation? In a world in which lifestyle indicates who people are the answer must be a resounding yes!

Uniqueness is not a license to anarchy or for everyone to do their own thing. The context of the Christian life is first and foremost that we are not our own. First Corinthians 6:19, 20 says: "What? Know ye not that your body is the temple of the Holy Ghost which is in you, which ye have of God, and ye are not your own? For ye are bought with a price: therefore glorify God in your body, and in your spirit, which are God's."

This passage sets the parameters for culture and lifestyle as does 1 Corinthians 10:31: "Whether therefore ye eat, or drink, or whatsoever ye do, do all to the glory of God." Philippians 4:8 adds: "Finally, brethren, whatsoever things are true, whatsoever things are honest, whatsoever things are just, whatsoever things are pure, whatsoever things are lovely, whatsoever things are of good report; if there be any virtue, and if there be any praise, think on these things."

Within the guidelines of these scriptures we find outlined a culture different from every other culture existing on our planet. As children of God we cannot survive the risk of being reabsorbed into the cultures of this world unless we insist on a unique identity. It is not necessary that our unique lifestyle be a matter of right or wrong. It is sufficient that it is different. In the framework of the great struggle between good and evil swirling around us it is necessary that we can be distinguished from the rest of the world.

During wartime the uniform a soldier wears is not a moral issue, but it is one of life and death, because it shows which side he or she is on. If people who are child molesters identified themselves by wearing orange neckties, you may be sure that although there is nothing intrinsically wrong with an orange necktie, I would not own one under those conditions.

Scripture is clear. As His sons and daughters God calls upon us not to conform to the culture and lifestyle of the world. Instead, He wants to transform us by renewing our minds so that we may do His will (Rom. 12:2).

Several other texts warn us that we can put ourselves in situations that may endanger our salvation. One tells us not to love the world or whatever belongs to it, and that if we persist in doing so, it will destroy our love for God (1 John 2:15). Another declares that those who insist on loving the world will eventually become God's enemies (James 4:4).

We have solved the question of how we are saved—through the divine gift of grace through faith (Eph. 2:8). What we must urgently address now is the matter of how a saved person then lives.

## What Is Important to Know

1. Our culture is the way we live. It is our lifestyle.

2. The Christian lifestyle will necessarily be different from that of a person not yet saved.

3. Some lifestyle elements are not a matter of morals but of identity. They maintain the identity of the group or family.

4. As long as we continue to let the prevailing culture determine our identity, the Holy Spirit will not be able to fulfill God's plan that we all have the character of Jesus.

## Personal Application

1. What does it mean to be in the world but not of the world?

2. What are some of the specific ways in which the prevailing culture wars with the lifestyle that Jesus modeled?

### Prayer

Heavenly Father, we think of Jesus' prayer in which He asked the Father to keep us from evil even though we still remain in the world. This is our prayer also. We see ourselves surrounded by cultures and values that oppose Your kingdom. In the past we were part of such cultures. Now, Lord, we see our need to develop a new way of life.

Although we know how to live in our respective cultures, we need to learn how to live a heavenly lifestyle and speak the language of heaven. Inasmuch as we are looking forward to spending eternity with You in Your culture, acclimate us now so that people can recognize at a glance that we belong to a heavenly country by the way we dress, talk, and worship.

We are thankful that You have given us Your Word and the Holy Spirit, which will produce those changes in us. Lord, we might suffer some culture shock in the process but may it all be to Your honor and glory through our Lord and Saviour Jesus Christ. Amen.

# *Expect to Pray Better*

One of the most important components of the Christian life is prayer. When we study the lives of victorious Christians, no matter when they lived, whether they were men or women, rich or poor, or whatever particular talent they happened to have, the one thing they had in common was that they were people of prayer.

Recently prayer has become a fad. Most people claim to be "spiritual" and report that they pray—and not only that, they claim God answers their prayers—from winning prize fights to football games. (God would probably decline most of the credit He receives for answering so many different kinds of prayers.)

People tell stories about how powerful prayer is and how through prayer they were able to get this or that in the nick of time. Such reports make just about everyone willing to give prayer a try. I hope I am not wrong when I say that I have concluded that prayer is not powerful. Rather, God is powerful. Even a weak prayer can reach our powerful God. We don't need 50,000 watts of pure prayer power in order to enter the presence of the Almighty. Prayer is not to be an end in itself, but a means to an end. It enables us to reach out and touch a powerful God as even a baby can touch its mother.

For this reason it is not necessary to learn some kind of prayer technique. It is not a certain kind of prayer or prayer technique that touches God's heart but rather the attitude of the person praying that really matters.

Most people believe that the more we pray, the better. I am sure there is something to that. On the other hand, I would rather pray right than pray much. As you will learn in this chapter, I am convinced it is possible both to pray right and to pray wrong. I am not talking about techniques or the words we use but the attitudes we have as we pray. They will shape what we expect from prayer.

Our prayers reflect our attitudes, and consequently they indicate the kinds of people we are. For this reason it is possible to look at what we are praying about or not praying about and discover who we really are.

The Bible speaks often of prayer. My computer concordance indicates 737 references in the King James Version to either "prayer," "pray," "prayed," or "praying." Of course, not all of these refer to praying to God. In Elizabethan English "pray" means to request something from someone. So I could say, "I pray you, come over to my house for dinner tomorrow." Nevertheless, prayer to God by certain people, at particular times, and with what results is a major theme in Scripture.

When we look closely at the prayers recorded in Scripture we find them typical of certain types of people who pray today. In this chapter we will look at several examples. We won't have to be Greek or Hebrew scholars to see ourselves in some of these illustrations. As an elderly man I used to work for liked to say, "People is people and folks is folks."

Pharaoh represents one type of person who prays (or in this case a person who requests prayer). The Hebrews had become slaves working on all kinds of public projects. Moses approached the Egyptian king and asked him to let the people go free, but Pharaoh refused. And so a chain of events began that would eventually leave the country in ruins. The Bible records them as the 10 plagues of Egypt.

As the plagues began to strike, things went from bad to worse. Several times the Pharaoh requested that Moses pray for him and his people. "Then Pharaoh called for Moses and Aaron in haste; and he said, I have sinned against the Lord your God, and against you. Now therefore forgive, I pray thee, my sin only this once, and entreat the Lord your God, that He may take away from me this death only" (Ex. 10:16, 17).

On the surface it appeared as though he had a true change of heart. He even admitted he had done wrong, confessing that he had sinned against God and against Moses. When he said, "Pray, just this once," he sounded genuinely sorry. It appeared as though he intended to put the past behind him and turn over a new leaf.

Pharaoh represents the person who comes under tremendous conviction and asks God to do something for them just to stop whatever in their life is upsetting things. I believe that from time to time genuine conversions come out of the proverbial foxhole, but we might not want to do a study of how many people ignore all they have promised the Lord once things get back to normal.

This is not to say that we shouldn't make promises when we are in trouble, but it is definitely to our advantage to follow through on them. Deuteronomy 23:21 declares: "When thou shalt vow a vow unto the Lord thy God, thou shalt not slack to pay it: for the Lord thy God will surely require it of thee; and it would be sin in thee." God does not take lightly the promises we make to Him.

Another group mentioned in Scripture who prayed were the hypocrites. In Matthew 6:5, Jesus urges us: "And when thou prayest, thou shalt not be as the hypocrites are: for they love to pray standing in the synagogues and in the corners of the streets, that they may be seen of men. Verily I say unto you, They have their reward."

Jesus is the first person in the Bible to use the word "hypocrite." That word in the Greek language meant actor. Actors pretend to be someone they are not. It isn't hard to imagine what the problem is with this kind of attitude in prayer.

Some people use prayer as a smoke screen. It makes them look as though they are religious when they really are not. One wonders if anyone else can tell when a person is being a hypocrite in their prayers, though probably their families know.

The hardest place of all to be a Christian is at home. People will often go to church and appear to be religious. They may even hold an office in the church, standing up front and proclaiming, "Aren't we glad that we are part of the family of God?" And there sit in the congregation the spouse and children who think to themselves, *Look who's talking. Who does he [she] think he's [she's] kidding?*

Jesus tells us that being up front and praying in public is no substitute for a personal devotional life. We can do that and still be a hypocrite. But if we spend time alone with Jesus in prayer on a regular basis, we may still have weaknesses to cope with, but our family will not regard us as a hypocrite, since we will not behave as two different people.

Perhaps you might be thinking that it would be better for us not to pray up front anymore, just to avoid the appearance of hypocrisy. But that would only make it worse. What would be better is to add to our public prayer some private time with God. It will make the life we live in front of everyone consistent with our private life. The biggest beneficiaries of the time we spend alone with God will be the members of our own families.

Jesus pointed out another attitude incompatible with the true spirit of prayer. He tells about a Pharisee who prayed and thanked God that he was not like other people. The Pharisee announced to God in his prayer how good he was and reminded Him about all the good things that he did (Luke 18:11, 12).

Perhaps the Pharisee didn't think he really needed to pray. But on the other hand, I suppose some might find nothing wrong with what he said, because he was only giving thanks to God for all his blessings. In the modern context we would say that the Pharisee had a high sense of self-esteem, and that his self-image was very healthy (by the way, you might be interested to know they have done studies on hardened criminals and discovered they typically have an extremely high sense of self-esteem).

Another thought that comes to mind when we read the Pharisee's prayer is that we are only as good as the people we compare ourselves with. As we have read before in 2 Corinthians 10:12: "For we dare not make ourselves of the number, or compare ourselves with some that commend themselves: but they measuring themselves by themselves, and comparing themselves among themselves, are not wise." The point of the passage is easy to grasp. When we want to make ourselves look good, we will usually compare ourselves with those whom we consider to be inferior. But Scripture says that is not a good idea.

It is perfectly all right to compare ourselves with Jesus. The good part of that is that when we do, two things happen. First, we realize that we are all on the same level in relationship to Him. As they say, the ground at the foot of the cross is level. And second, although comparing ourselves with Jesus will initially cut us down to size, He then picks us up, just as He declares that those who humble themselves shall be exalted, and those who exalt themselves will be abased (Matt. 23:12). We studied this concept in more detail in chapter 5.

Another attitude of a person who prays appears in Luke 18:13: "And the publican, standing afar off, would not lift up so much as his eyes unto heaven, but smote upon his breast, saying, God be merciful to me a sinner."

You may be aware that the publicans were tax collectors for the Roman occupation government. To be a publican was to be immediately associated with everything bad, a traitor to one's people and dishonest to the core. That wasn't necessarily true, however. Scripture refers to two publicans who were good people: Matthew, who wrote the first book of the New Testament, and Zacchaeus, the short man who climbed up a tree to get a good view of Jesus and who then came down when Jesus invited Himself over for dinner.

Notice the self-concept the publican expressed in his prayer. He might have prayed the following:

"Dear Lord, You know people are really on my case. They are trying to put me down all the time. I know that any of them would do what I do for a living if they were smart enough, but they didn't receive the breaks that I got and so they are just jealous. Help me to hang in there, Lord, because I know I am as good as any one of them. Amen."

But that was not his attitude. From our modern perspective he exhibited a very low self-esteem. The way Jesus describes the man it might make you think he must have carried a heavy load of guilt, which to some in this day and age would be a symptom of dysfunction.

What happens in his prayer is important to understand, and we need to take the matter seriously, because it flies in the face of a lot of what people teach and believe today. The publican doesn't sound like a person immersed in himself or one who loved himself first. Notice what Jesus said was God's view of the publican. "I tell you, this man went down to his house justified" (verse 14).

Some claim that we need to affirm ourselves every chance we get. However, Jesus said if we take that attitude into our prayers, we will be in for a big surprise. Remember, sin got its start from positive self-talk. Lucifer said: "I will ascend into heaven, I will exalt my throne above the stars of God: I will sit also upon the mount of the congregation, in the sides of the north: I will ascend above the heights of the clouds; I will be like the most High" (Isa. 14:13, 14). The proud and selfish don't need what God has to offer inasmuch as they are pretty much their own gods.

Our attitude in prayer is everything. "But the Lord said unto Samuel, Look not on his countenance, or on the height of his stature; because I have refused him: for the Lord seeth not as man seeth; for man looketh on the outward appearance, but the Lord looketh on the heart" (1 Sam. 16:7).

At times it may be not only wrong to pray but actually useless. A case study appears in Joshua 7:6 that tells what happened after the battle of Ai. "Joshua rent his clothes, and fell to the earth upon his face before the ark of the Lord until the eventide, he and the elders of Israel, and put dust upon their heads." Notice how the Lord reacted to his apparently fervent prayer. "Get thee up; wherefore liest thou thus upon thy face? Israel hath sinned, and they have also transgressed my covenant which I commanded them. . . . Up, sanctify the people, and say, Sanctify yourselves . . . There is an accursed thing in the midst of thee" (verses 10-13).

There is a time to pray and a time to act on what we are praying about. It is right to pray that the Lord will bless us and do great things in our lives, but the bottom line is that there comes a time in which we must get off our knees and begin to implement in our lives what we have been praying about.

One morning as I was having my devotions, I heard a knock at the door and the voice of my granddaughter say, "Grandpa, can I come in?"

For a moment I thought I would tell her she should come back later, as I was busy. Then it occurred to me that one of the reasons I was praying was so that I would be a better grandfather to the little girl. It was time to stop praying and start putting what I had been praying about into practice.

Who prays? The Bible offers many examples of men and women who prayed. They were all kinds of people, and they prayed in all kinds of circumstances for all kinds of things.

We may expect that a successful Christian life rests on prayer. But prayer is not about techniques or using certain words. The Christian prayer life is, in the final analysis, about attitudes. It is possible to pray for all the right things but for all the wrong reasons. Because of this, we must first of all pray that the Lord, who alone knows what we are really like, will reveal to us what we need most. I suspect that most of us require a change of attitude, and that can come only from a change of heart.

It is for this reason God's invitation to us is always to use the words of Proverbs 23:26, "My son, give me thine heart." That is why our main concern every day should be to make sure our heart is right with God.

I invite you to do a reality check on your prayers. Not so that you will stop praying, but rather that by God's grace you will pray better. We will all pray better as we allow God to change us. David had it right when he prayed: "Create in me a clean heart, O God; and renew a right spirit within me" (Ps. 51:10).

---

### What Is Important to Know

1. God is not impressed with the techniques of prayer.

2. Sometimes we can actually be praying for the right things but for the wrong reasons.

3. On the other hand, we also could conceivably be praying for the wrong things but for the right reasons. Therefore we must discover from Scripture what we should pray about.

4. We need to recognize that we cannot ask God to do something in our lives and then just sit back and watch it happen. Prayer doesn't take us out of the loop—it puts us into it but on the Lord's side.

---

### Personal Application

1. Why is humility a prerequisite for effective prayer?

2. Review what you have been praying about recently. Are you cooperating with the Lord so that He might be able to answer your prayers? What can you do to enhance your participation?

---

### Prayer

Father, we are thankful that You have invited us to talk to You. The trouble is that we sometimes try to use You to get our will done rather than asking that Your will be done. Occasionally we want You to do everything so that we don't have to do anything. Thank You for Your patience with us. We need patience too. Lord, teach us to pray so that when we talk to You we are on the same wavelength. In Jesus' name, amen.

# Expect to Be Perfect in Christ

One point of view declares it is impossible to be perfect. Another position believes that we must be perfect before Jesus can come. Taken together, these views have made any discussion of Christian perfection a no-no in polite Christian circles.

Yet we shouldn't neglect to talk about perfection, because Scripture is full of the word. "I am the Almighty God; walk before me, and be thou perfect" (Gen. 17:1). "Thou shalt be perfect with the Lord thy God" (Deut. 18:13). "Let your heart therefore be perfect with the Lord our God" (1 Kings 8:61). "The eyes of the Lord run to and fro throughout the whole earth, to shew himself strong in the behalf of them whose heart is perfect toward him" (2 Chron. 16:9). "I will behave myself wisely in a perfect way" (Ps. 101:2). "The Lord will perfect that which concerneth me" (Ps. 138:8). "The disciple is not above his master: but every one that is perfect shall be as his master" (Luke 6:40). "Let us cleanse ourselves from all filthiness of the flesh and spirit, perfecting holiness in the fear of God" (2 Cor. 7:1). "Be perfect" (2 Cor. 13:11). "Christ in you, the hope of glory: whom we preach, warning every man, and teaching every man in all wisdom; that we may present every man perfect in Christ Jesus" (Col. 1:27, 28). "Labouring fervently for you in prayers, that ye may stand perfect and complete in all the will of God" (Col. 4:12). "Therefore leaving the principles of the doctrine of Christ, let us go on unto perfection" (Heb. 6:1). "Now the God of peace . . . make you perfect in every good work to do his will" (Heb. 13:20, 21). "Let patience have her perfect work, that ye may be perfect and entire, wanting in nothing" (James 1:4). "But the God of all grace . . . make you perfect, stablish, strengthen, settle you" (1 Peter 5:10).

Not only does the Scripture call us to perfection, but it speaks about people who were perfect. The first person to have the word perfect applied to him was Noah. Genesis 6:9 says that "Noah was a just man and perfect in his generations, and Noah walked with God." Later in Genesis we find that this perfect man who walked with God was also the one who whipped up a little home brew and got drunk.

The Bible calls Job perfect. God Himself described him as a perfect and upright man (Job 1:1). But he must not have had it all together yet, because Job himself said, "I abhor myself, and repent in dust and ashes" (Job 42:6).

First Kings 11:4 speaks of David having a heart "perfect with the Lord." Let's not even talk about his deeds. In addition to his sin with Bathsheba, he was a guerrilla fighter for years, and as a father his record wasn't so good either. Another man referred to in Scripture as perfect was King Asa. It is said of him that his heart "was perfect with the Lord all his days" (1 Kings 15:14).

Referring to such men as perfect while looking at some of the things they did makes the Bible appear to contradict itself. But when Scripture speaks of them as perfect, it is not focusing on their ways, because from time to time they made mistakes. It has in mind their hearts, describing them as having a heart perfect before the Lord. A heart wholly consecrated to God and dedicated to fellowship with

Him is a perfect heart. A person whose heart is wholly for God is a perfect human being.

Scripture describes God's perfect ones who have made a perfect commitment as being in the process of being perfected (Phil. 3:13-15). A person with a perfect heart will pray and strive to be perfect in practice as well. How can a person who is totally committed to God desire anything less than to perfectly do His will?

The psalmist says: "I will delight to do Thy precepts. With my whole heart will I observe Thy law" (Ps. 40:8, paraphrased). With our hearts perfect before Him, we will desire to perfectly do His will. We will long to be obedient.

Not only are we perfect in our commitment while being perfected day by day, but this process will never end. "The years of eternity, as they roll, will bring richer and still more glorious revelations of God and of Christ. As knowledge is progressive, so will love, reverence, and happiness increase" (Ellen G. White, *The Great Controversy*, p. 678).

Our problem is that sin has led us to see the abnormal as normal and to accept the unacceptable. We have become so accustomed to our imperfection that we actually defend selfishness, pride, lust, criticism, and the lack of self-control that many see as normal, or if not normal, as permanent disabilities that we somehow must live with in spite of the personal and social devastation they cause. God created humanity perfect in His image. He will not be satisfied until He has restored to us the perfection that Adam and Eve lost in Eden. The Bible writers were not satisfied with the status quo. I will not be content either.

It is incredible, but many desire to have a perfect figure, get a perfect job, or be a perfect basketball player, but in the Christian life they don't try to be perfect or they say they don't believe it is possible.

It is the goal of perfection that gives hope and direction to the Christian life. A person who doesn't know where they are going won't realize it when they wander off the road. How can we have target practice unless we have a target?

Of course, we must avoid the extreme positions that often result from what we refer to as "perfectionism." Some have said they have seen perfectionism slay its thousands. That may be true, but imperfectionism has slain its ten thousands. Many soothe themselves by saying that nobody is perfect. Sadly, they make little progress in the Christian walk because they have never known that they can serve God with a perfect heart and that a perfect heart is the secret to a perfect way.

The problem that many sincere Christians have with the doctrine of Christian perfection is that it seems to clash with the great truth of justification by faith. But when properly understood it does not. Perfection is a fruit of what Jesus has done for us through His death and resurrection (Rom. 5:10).

A few years ago I mulled over the concept of perfection in light of the fact that it so easily divides Christians when it is actually a great truth that should unite us. I happen to keep a journal. In trying to resolve the tension between the two points of view, I wrote the following, which has helped me to understand some of the issues involved: "There is a difference between Godlikeness and being gods. God's perfection is the way He is intrinsically. In Him is life unborrowed and underived. Our life is and always will be borrowed and derived. In Him we live and move and have our being (Acts 17:28). And this is going to be our permanent state. Even when we get to heaven we will always have to eat from the tree of life (Rev. 22:2). God's work in our life is always a perfect one. He saw what He made, and behold it was very good. His work in our lives is perfect, yet He continues to perfect us.

"Some have stated that Jesus will come when His people perfectly reflect His character. We emphasize the word 'perfectly' and sometimes overlook the significance of the word 'reflect.' We must never forget that we will always be only reflectors. He is the sun; we are the moon. The moon gives a perfect reflection of the sun because it reflects the sun and the sun only. Yet it is not a total reflection of the sun. The sun still has more light than the moon can reflect. Yet the moon itself reflects all of the sun it can, given its size and distance from it. Obviously, if the moon were nearer to the sun, it would reflect more of its light.

"The moon cannot become a sun because of its nature. It has no light in itself and must be content to be a reflector. To perfectly reflect the character of Christ means that it will be His character that we reflect and not that of anyone else. Yet it will always be less than Christ, because it will always be a reflection, albeit unobstructed. As moons are of different sizes, so we as individuals are different. The reflection of Christ in the lives of His people throughout the ages is always influenced by their 'size and distance' from the Son. Yet the reflection is always perfect because Jesus, the perfect Sun of righteousness, is the source of the light. Though we don't all reflect the same amount of light, like Noah and David of old we serve Him with a perfect heart.

"We must always bear in mind that perfection is not established by being compared with something that is imperfect. Something is called perfect because of its relationship to the standard, not to the broken or inferior.

"Perfection in the Christian life has to do with the Christian's relationship to God and His holiness, not with his relationship to sin and the devil. Sin is another issue. The goal of the Christian life is not simply to be sinless but to be holy in Christ. 'Be not conformed to this world: but be ye transformed by the renewing of your mind, that ye may prove what is that good, and acceptable, and perfect, will of God' (Rom. 12:2). Victorious Christian living, therefore, is a means to an end and not an end in itself. Because of this, we must always see sin as an enemy, because just as the moon's relationship to the earth will affect its ability to reflect the sun, so our relationship to the earth will affect our ability to reflect the Sun of righteousness."

I have seven grandchildren. The newest one is a year old. Just learning to walk, she cannot talk or feed herself or care for even her most basic needs, yet she is perfect. Not as perfect as she will be as she grows and develops, but as perfect as she needs to be given how old she is. She was born perfect, she is being perfected, and one day she will be perfect. Do you see? To those of us who are sons and daughters of God with our hearts perfect toward Him, He is working in us both to will and to do His good pleasure (Phil. 2:13). And best of all, we have the promise that "He which hath begun a good work in you will perform it until the day of Jesus Christ" (Phil. 1:6).

So let's not fight perfection, but go on to perfection. A perfect God can demand no less than perfection from His people. "Faithful is he that calleth you, who also will do it" (1 Thess. 5:24). Let us expect to be perfect in Christ.

### What Is Important to Know

1. God calls His people in every generation to perfection.

2. The Bible refers to Noah, Job, David, and Asa as being perfect. Though they were not perfect in deed, they were "perfect in heart."

3. A person who serves the Lord with a perfect heart will strive daily to serve Him perfectly in deed.

4. We are perfect while we are being perfected. Though we are now perfect in Christ, we are not as perfect as we will be in the future.

### Personal Application

1. What do you think it means to serve God with a perfect heart?

2. What areas of your life need to reflect more of Jesus' character? What would you have to remove to make this possible?

### Prayer

Holy Father, forgive us for our lack of faith. Forgive us for not believing that You who have begun Your work in us can finish it. You are not only the author but the finisher of our faith. We give our lives to You in perfect commitment—all that we know we are today. Now, O Holy Spirit, continue to perfect us. Not just here and now, not just today or tomorrow, but may this be the beginning of bathing our souls in Your holiness forever and ever, world without end. Amen and amen.

# Expect to Have the Blessed Hope

A number of years ago a large metropolitan church invited me to teach the Sabbath school lesson. That Sabbath they decided not to divide into classes but to have one general lesson study.

The theme of the lessons that quarter had been last-day events and the coming of Jesus. The lesson I had been assigned to teach that Sabbath had to do with the actual event of the second coming of Jesus.

After trying to think about what I could share that might be new and relevant, I decided that instead of reviewing what they already knew about the return of Jesus I would ask them how they felt about it. I have noticed that what a person knows about something may be one thing but how they feel about it may be completely different. So I made up a little questionnaire. Since I did not put the questions together in a scientific way, I am not able to say the results were accurate plus or minus a certain percentage. That wasn't the point. The idea was to give the people a chance to discover how they felt about Jesus' second coming.

Before I share with you the questions and the responses, I want you to know that I have since asked essentially the same core questions in South America and in Africa, and believe it or not, I received the same answers as those from that first Sabbath school class that day.

The first question was: "Do you want Jesus to come?" I realized that a questionnaire is usually multiple choice, and when you ask a question like this you should give several possible answers. So I tried to give all the choices I could think of. The possible responses were "Yes," "No," "Very much," and "Explain." The second question was "If you could set a date for His coming, when would it be?" When the class saw that question several raised their hands to comment that we can't know the day or the hour. I explained I was aware of that, but the question was not trying to set a date—rather it was suggesting that if it were up to us to decide when Jesus would come, when would we want it to be? The purpose of my questionnaire, of course, was to help them see how they felt about the whole subject. There were other questions, but the last one put a finger on our feelings, because it asked: "When Jesus comes, will you be ready?"

The responses were revealing. To the first question, "Do you want Jesus to come?" no one answered "No." It didn't really tell much about how a person felt about the coming of Jesus. But the second question was a different matter. It asked, "If you could set a date for His coming, when would it be?"

Some time before, I had asked this question to a group of young people in South America at a day academy. As did the people in the United States they too said they wanted Jesus to come. But instead of asking them if they could set a date for His coming, I inquired if they wanted Jesus to come before they got married or after.

You can probably guess how the young people responded. Though they virtually all expressed that they wanted Jesus to come, they were almost unanimous in wanting Him to wait until after they got married.

The young people were honest. Of course, to a married person that question would not be a concern. Yet those of us who are married have our own reasons for not wanting Jesus to return just yet. Have you noticed that if you lose your job, you want Him to come more than when you get a raise or a promotion? We want Jesus to appear when we are being evicted from our apartment, or when the furnace breaks down; but when we are building a new house we have been planning for many years, we may say, "Lord, couldn't You wait just till I finish my house? I want to move in at least."

Nearly everyone in Sabbath school that day put a date for the coming of Jesus that ranged from 5 to 20 years in the future. I could tell who the exceptions were by their shaky handwriting. As long as we have a bit of health and a bit of money and things are going well, our unspoken prayer is "Lord, don't be in a hurry."

The last question in the survey revealed even deeper feelings. It asked, "When Jesus comes, will you be ready?" The choices for answer were"Yes," "No," "I hope so," and "I don't know."

Most of the people checked "I hope so." They were not sure. If you are going to take a trip somewhere and you are packed, have your ticket, and are all ready to go, and someone asks if you are going on a trip, you probably wouldn't answer "I hope so."

Why couldn't we just say yes to that question? Could it be because we wonder if we are ready? I think we have mixed feelings about the return of Jesus because it is like the old saying "A bird in the hand is worth two in the bush." We know how we are now, and we know what we have, but when we think of the second advent of Jesus we don't have a clear idea of what might happen to us.

As far as our planet is concerned the return of Jesus will be catastrophic. It will leave earth a broken ruin. So it is no wonder that deep down in our hearts we have so many mixed feelings about it. We are not sure we want it to happen, because we could be lost, our spouse could be lost, or our children could be lost.

We used to hear lots of sermons about the coming of Jesus. During the Cuban missile crisis in the 1960s, when the ships from Russia loaded with missiles steamed toward Cuba, I received a letter from a young woman that said, "Pastor, please go visit my mother. She hasn't given her life to Jesus, and He is coming."

As I look back I can see that God's people have gone through many disappointments since 1844. We have packed and unpacked for the coming of Jesus so many times it is hard to get excited about it anymore. As a result we have generally lost what the Bible refers to as the "blessed hope" (Titus 2:13). You see, there is a vast difference between the signs of Jesus' coming and the blessed hope. The signs tell us where we are in relationship to His coming, while the blessed hope is how we feel about it.

Through the years some of us have used the signs of His coming as a club to threaten each other. "You had better be good, Jesus is coming!" That will work a few times, but when He doesn't return, that approach ceases to be effective. Like those to whom the little boy cried wolf, people stop believing what we are saying and don't respond anymore. In a similar way many have become desensitized to the Second Coming.

It is interesting to note that this is the way the Scriptures said it would be. The parable in Matthew 25:1-13 tells of 10 young women who wanted to be there when the bridegroom brought the bride home to live with him. In that part of the world the groom is the center of attention, so they weren't bridesmaids but groomsmaids! The groom didn't come when expected (it is bad manners in the Middle East to rush such important matters), so everyone in the wedding party went to sleep. While they slept the groom approached. They woke up at the last minute, and half of them discovered that they had run out of oil for their little lamps.

Five had extra oil with them, and five had to run to buy more. While they were gone the procession moved on. When the five unprepared maids arrived at the groom's home he wouldn't let them in (verse 12).

I like to think the oil represents the Holy Spirit (1 Sam. 16:13). The Holy Spirit is what leads us to love Jesus and look forward to

His coming. Threatening people doesn't make anyone love anyone else. A scare or a threat cannot produce love. If my wife were to tell me I had better love her or she is going to hit me over the head with a rolling pin, do you think that would make me feel more affection toward her?

Some recognize that for all intents and purposes they have gone to sleep spiritually, but they figure that when the signs really heat up, their lamps will suddenly reignite. We should not expect it to happen.

World events, wars, or earthquakes will not generate love for Jesus and a desire for His return. Such things may shake us up and frighten us badly. We may change our outward lives from pure adrenaline, but adrenaline will not alter the heart. Threatening does not transform it. Only the Holy Spirit can do that.

It seems as though the majority of those waiting for Jesus to come have drifted off to sleep. It is a fulfillment of Scripture. The part that is sobering is what is happening to us as we sleep, and it is that we may very well be losing the blessed hope.

I invite you to look into your heart. I don't ask you what you know about the coming of Jesus, but I urge you to examine how you feel about it. I also raise the question that I presented to the Sabbath school class that day: "When Jesus comes, will you be ready?"

How will you know if you are ready? When you have given all your heart to Jesus—not the way you used to be, or the way you wish you were, but just what you are. When you start your day tomorrow and every day thereafter, get down on your knees and say, "Jesus, I want to give You what I am. Take me today just as I am." And then ask Him to begin to fill your heart with His love and your life with His Holy Spirit. Pray for the fruit of the Spirit. If you are doing that, if you are giving your heart to Him every day, then if someone asks if you will be ready when Jesus comes, you can answer yes!

Knowing He is getting us ready and has promised that He will finish the work He has begun in our hearts changes our whole perspective. Who wants to go out and tell others that Jesus will return if secretly we hope it won't happen? Or who longs to hurry the coming of Jesus if we feel that we might be lost?

Jacob had to work seven years to earn the right to marry Rachel, but the Scripture says those seven years went quickly because he loved her so much (Gen. 29:20). When we have the blessed hope our waiting for the coming of Jesus will not drag out, but time will race past because we love Him so much.

When the apostle Paul described the resurrection he said, "We which are alive and remain" (1 Thess. 4:15). Paul didn't have the assurance he would still be alive when Jesus came, but he hoped so.

John ends the book of Revelation with words of the blessed hope. "Even so, come, Lord Jesus" (Rev. 22:20).

The blessed hope is what results when we make Jesus the Lord of our life, when we put all on the altar of sacrifice, when we love neither the world nor what belongs to it. Then suddenly the coming of Jesus begins to mean everything. And although you and I don't know the day or the hour of His coming, still, if someone asks us the question "When Jesus returns, will you be ready?" we will say, "Oh, yes!" Things will change for us when we feel that way. What a glorious day it will be when within our hearts and within the body of Christ we again have the blessed hope!

---

### What Is Important to Know

1. What we know about something and how we feel about it may be two different things.

2. When things are going well or when we have something special that we want to accomplish we tend to want to put off the Second Coming.

3. The parable of the 10 virgins basically tells us that everyone who is waiting for the coming of Jesus goes to sleep.

4. It is the Holy Spirit that gets us ready for the return of Jesus, not threats or fear, although these things could conceivably wake us up.

## Personal Application

1. As you have read this last chapter in the book I invite you to give serious thought to how you feel about the coming of Jesus and why. As you contemplate the second advent of our Lord, what is your prayer?

2. Scripture teaches that love of the world and love for God are incompatible. What should be our relationship to this world and its culture?

## Prayer

O Father, we have waited so long for the coming of Jesus. While it thrills us, it also frightens us. Lord, we don't know the day or the hour. But it doesn't really matter. We know that our names are written in heaven and that You who have begun a good work in us have promised to finish it.

The Bible assures us that You are not willing that any should perish. You can understand, then, some of our feelings when we have unsaved loved ones. While You have promised to give us a crown and Jesus has prepared mansions for us, Father, it is not so much the crowns or the mansions we want as that You save our children and our grandchildren—our families, Lord. You are the one who made families. We plead with You to do whatever You must to save our families!

Forgive us where we ourselves have been stumbling blocks to the salvation of others. We want to be Your sons and daughters, in whom You are well pleased. Forgive us for going to sleep and loving the things of the world more than the things of Your eternal kingdom.

Lord, like Jacob of old, we will not let You go until You bless us. In Jesus' name, amen.